The
Selected
Poems of
Paul
Blackburn

Persea Lamplighter Titles
Essential Texts in Poetry and Poetics
M. L. Rosenthal, General Editor

Other books by Paul Blackburn

The Dissolving Fabric (1955)
Brooklyn-Manhattan Transit (1960)
The Nets (1961)
The Cities (1967)
In . On . Or About the Premises (1968)
Early Selected Y Mas (1972)
The Journals (1975)
Halfway Down the Coast (1975)
Against the Silences (1980)
The Collected Poems of Paul Blackburn (1985)
The Parallel Voyages (1987)

Selected Translations by Paul Blackburn

Poem of the Cid (1966)
End of the Game and Other Stories, by Julio Cortazar (1967)
Hunk of Skin, by Pablo Picasso (1968)
Cronopios and Famas, by Julio Cortazar (1969)
Proensa: An Anthology of Troubadour Poetry (1978)
Lorca/Blackburn (1979)

The Selected Poems of Paul Blackburn

edited, with
an introduction, by
Edith Jarolim

Persea Books • New York

Persea Books
60 Madison Avenue
New York, N.Y. 10010

Library of Congress Cataloging in Publication Data

Blackburn, Paul.
  The selected poems of Paul Blackburn.

    I. Jarolim, Edith.   II. Title.
PS3552.L342A6   1989   811'.54   88-7933
ISBN 0-89255-123-2 (pbk.)

The publication of this book was made possible in part by a grant from the National Endowment for the Arts.

Designed by Peter St. John Ginna
Set in Electra by Keystrokes, Lenox, Massachusetts

Printed in the United States of America

First Printing

For Carlos

Foreword

Welcome to Paul Blackburn's selected poems. Don't stop to prepare yourself in any way. Just come right in and you'll be with him at once on some New York or Barcelona street, it may be, or in McSorley's tavern near the Bowery, or overlooking the sea in Málaga, or in some shared or lonely bedroom, or wherever. As for what comes next, the poem will draw you further into itself: i.e., toward whatever musings have been set ticking right there in the middle of things:

> It's going to rain
> Across the avenue a crane
> whose name is
>   CIVETTA LINK-BELT
> dips, rises and turns in a
>   graceless geometry
>
>   But grace is slowness / as
> ecstasy is some kind of speed or madness /
> The crane moves slowly, that
> much is graceful / The men
>   watch and the leaves

Thus begins the poem called "The Watchers." Natural, confiding speech conspires easily with the simple opening rhyme—genially inviting, like a friend's quick summons to look at something interesting that's happening on the street. And before we know it, the huge machine with the felinely technical trade-name is almost personified, as if it were a dancer or a bird. (The phrasing recalls the seagull whose wings "dip and pivot him" in Hart Crane's "To Brooklyn Bridge.") Now the musings take over: thoughts about the crane's "graceless geometry" and, contrariwise, about the meaning of "grace" and—in an immensely suggestive associative leap (esthetic, psychological, sexual)—of "ecstasy." Then the poem returns to the literal scene, which has become charged with these resonances.

This is how Blackburn's art works: lightly, broodingly, absorbingly. The opening couplet of "The Watchers" takes us unawares. It is plain, casual. Its rhythm is off-center, with two stresses in the first line but three in the second; also, the second line creates a slight jolt, for it unexpectedly introduces a new sentence. These tiny imbalances quietly prepare the poem for its shifts soon afterward to more richly complex diction and rhythms. The ear at work here is remarkably attuned to both sophisticated and ordinary speech. Of all the successors to Pound and Williams, Blackburn comes closest to their ability to mix the colloquial and formal, and to their instinct for melodic patterning and for volatile improvisational immediacy:

> Flick of perfume, slight and faintly bitter
> on my wrist, where her hand had rested
>
> ("Remains of an Afternoon")

But one need only open this selection at random, to find more such lines. The pleasure and turmoil of life and awareness, depths of sun-warmed tranquility but also of depression, degrees of passion both sensual and exalted— all these are the stuff of Blackburn's uninhibited expression. He was the poet of New York, city of poets, as it is today, and at the same time a student of the troubadours. His idiom ranges from gross street talk to whatever the lyric tradition can offer a writer whose mind plays joyously with styles and tonalities that have enchanted his reverie since childhood. Blackburn was that sort of poet, an American original who knew and loved what he was doing.

M.L. Rosenthal

Contents

Introduction

Asked to write a biographical statement for one of his last books of poems, Paul Blackburn described himself this way: "A New Englander by birth, a Westerner by accident, and a New Yorker by trade, he is Mediterranean by adoption . . . And he writes these poems, see? Poor fellow." He qualified this typically self-ironic summation with a quote from the 12th century poet, Jaufre Raudel, one of the many Provençal troubadours whose work he translated: "I want pity from no one for a pain/ I would share with no man."

To the end, which came early, at the age of 44, the pain in Blackburn's poems was mitigated by the act of writing them, by the careful attention he paid to the most minor details of everyday life. Blackburn was surely formed by those places and circumstances he cites: that he was a New Englander, subject to a strict, even cruel, early upbringing, and that he believed in the value of work. That, son of a poet, he considered poetry a vocation, no less—and no more—important than the work others did. That he studied Provençal poetry and travelled to Spain early on, and learned that a poet such as Federico García-Lorca may be revered by ordinary working people. That he wrote poetry in New York City for most of his adult life, and brought his Mediterranean belief in the democracy of poetry and his New England belief in the usefulness of poetry to the poetry scene there, and became not only a quintessentially urban poet, but also one of the most generous and genuinely committed writers to have ever appeared on that scene.

Born in St. Albans, Vermont, on November 24, 1926, Blackburn was raised there by his maternal grandparents from the age of 4, when his mother and father separated. His father headed west, to California. His mother, the poet Frances Frost, went first to Burlington and then to New York to try to make a living as a writer; when Paul was 14 years old, he was brought to live with her in Greenwich Village. Those who met him later in life were surprised to find he had studied at such American schools as New York University and then the University of Wisconsin—but it was at Wisconsin that he began reading Provençal poetry and corresponding with Ezra Pound, occasionally hitchhiking out to Washington, D.C., to visit him at St. Elizabeth's.

In his later poems, Blackburn came to wear his learning lightly; in his generally short early lyrics, his erudition is still on display. (Pound's example was not likely to have discouraged him in that regard.) The young man who wrote the lovely "Cantar de Noit" and satirical "For Mercury, Patron of Thieves: A Laurel" had clearly done his homework in Provençal and Greek poetics. But he was also taking lessons from such American masters as William Carlos Williams—and he was a natural when it came to picking up the rhythms of New York City streets:

> Th' holdup at the liquor-store, d'ja hear?
> a detective
> watch't 'm for ten minutes
> He took it anyway
> Got away down Broadway   Yeah?
> Yeah.
>
> ("The Continuity")

The way the poem had already begun to look on the page, a visual representation or "scoring" of the oral rendition of the poem, showed the influence too of another American poet, Charles Olson. On Pound's suggestion in 1951, Blackburn had written to a "chicken farmer in New Hampshire," Robert Creeley; Creeley in turn introduced him to the ideas and poetry of Olson. Although Blackburn always disliked putting poets into categories, and although he never set foot on the campus of Black Mountain College, he has come to be associated with Olson and the other writers who studied or taught at the experimental North Carolina school. If rather superficial, the "Black Mountain poet" label is not entirely misleading: Blackburn was New York distributor for the *Black Mountain Review*, the literary magazine established in 1953 to raise money for the floundering institution, and contributing editor to one of its issues. More to the point, of all those associated with the Black Mountain aesthetic, he was arguably the most skilled practitioner of the punctuation, line breaks, and text alignments that define the poetics of "composition by field," as outlined in Olson's 1951 "Projective Verse" essay.

In 1954, newly married and newly appointed Fulbright Teaching Fellow, Blackburn went off to Europe to study the language and literature of the troubadours. He never lost his interest in either, but he heartily hated Toulouse, the wet and provincial center of modern Provence (see his poem "Sirventes" against the city). During the two years he was assigned to teach in Toulouse, he escaped frequently to Spain, eventually settling there for a year. He loved that country's speech, which he heard on the streets and read in Lorca's poetry, the slow rhythms and living traditions of Mediterranean culture, and the nonsacredotal but anchoring rituals of everyday life:

You shall not always sit in sunlight watching
    weeds grow out of drainpipes
    or burros and shadows of burros
    come up the street bring sand
    the first one of the line with a
bell
Always.
    With a bell.

                    ("Suerte")

He was right about the limits of his European idyll. When he came back to New York in Fall 1957, ostensibly just to recoup finances, things rapidly fell apart: his marriage broke up, he couldn't find a job, and his mother died of cancer. But hiding out in Brooklyn from his ex-wife and commuting into Manhattan, he began writing the series of subway poems for which he is probably best known, including "Brooklyn Narcissus," "Clickety-Clack," and "Meditation on the BMT." And soon enough he found new loves, new rituals, and a new population for his street observations—the men crowded around the radio listening to the ball game, the secretary dreaming out the window of her office. Truly an urban representative, Blackburn could deftly enlarge the pain of his own situations to encompass wider political contexts, for example, the impingement of impersonal institutions on the individual's life:

After your voice's frozen anger
emptied the air between us, the
silence of electrical connections
the vacant window pale, the
connection broken : :

               ("AT&T Has My Dime")

By the mid-1960s his politics were more explicit in poems that criticized the U.S. presence in Vietnam ("Foreign Policy Commitments") or looked irreverently at the space program ("Newsclips 2."). But most of Blackburn's energies were devoted to his very nonpolitical activities on the poetry scene in New York. He returned in the late 1950s to find a burgeoning bard nouveau movement in town: poetry readings, sometimes to jazz accompaniment, were springing up in coffeehouses all over the city. He took part in some of these early mixed media programs and was instrumental in organizing two important Lower East Side reading series, at the Deux Megots Coffeehouse and later at Le Metro Cafe. It was Blackburn's idea in 1966 to move the readings at Le Metro to St. Mark's-Church-in-the-Bowery, where the Poetry Project still flourishes today.

It may be at the cost of his own fame that he devoted himself to spreading the word and encouraging the work of so many poets: translator of Julio Cortázar, Lorca, and the troubadours, among others, he also faithfully tape-recorded local poets at an astonishing number of readings, and gave countless fledgling writers aesthetic and practical advice. There are those who felt he spread himself too thin, dissipating his energies on writers unworthy of attention. Perhaps. But these activities very movingly attest to Blackburn's remarkable commitment to the ideal of a democratic community of poets.

And, for at least part of the decade anyway, Blackburn seemed to have energy to spare: he was at the height of his powers in the early to mid-1960s, producing, in addition to his political poems, such masterful mythic pieces as "The Watchers" and "At the Well." By mid-decade, however, the ambivalence about love, always a presence in the poems, became stronger, and the alert observing persona seems more a lonely voyeur, often sitting with other men in a bar and talking about the futility of love, or maybe not talking at all:

> It is March 9th, 3:30 in the afternoon
>
> The loudest sound in this public room
> is the exhaust fan in the east window
>   or the cat at my back
>   asleep there in the sun
>   bleached tabletop, golden
>   shimmer of ale   .
>
>   ("The Island")

In September 1967, his second marriage having broken up a few months earlier, a distraught and seemingly disconsolate Blackburn boarded the S.S. *Aurelia* for Europe. "The Glorious Morning," the account of the ensuing shipboard romance with his third-wife-to-be, marked Blackburn's first foray into the more loosely constructed, freewheeling records of daily life he came to call "journals." Although they were selective records, and his by-then ingrained sense of poetic form always kept them under aesthetic control, he distinguished them from the "poems" he continued to write during this period. He never felt entirely confident about the form, but it allowed him the space and latitude to write such long, cumulatively powerful pieces as "From the November Journals: Fire," as well as the freedom for such quick takes as "Along the San Andreas Fault."

A new, more flexible poetic style, a settled relationship, a first child, and a teaching job at the State University at Cortland, in northern New York—life seemed good in 1970, the year Blackburn learned that he had inoperable cancer of the esophagous. Up until a month before he died, on September 13, 1971, he continued to record, without self-pity and without denial, his honest reactions to the news: memories triggered of his body when he was 15 years old, of places he loved, and, characteristically, of poets and poetry and poems.

In the face of death his priorities remained the same—to keep observing, not only himself but also his surroundings, in which he continually saw things anew. Blackburn was too lustful, too urban, and too lapsed a Catholic to be

a very methodical spiritual seeker, but this self-described "Westerner by acci-
dent" always paid Zen-like attention to the thing itself, and often took comfort
in the notion of process, the equalizing principles of the universal flux and flow:

> All our farewells al-
> ready prepared inside us   . aaall our
> deaths we carry inside us, double-yolked, the
> fragile toughness of the shell . it makes
> sustenance possible, makes love   possible
> as the red buds break against the sunlight
> possible green, as legs move against legs
> possible softnesses   .

("Journal: April 19: The Southern Tier")

Edith Jarolim
New York, 1989

Editorial Note

The texts of these poems are those established for *The Collected Poems of Paul Blackburn* (Persea, 1985). All of them were previously published during the poet's lifetime or authorized by him for publication before his death. The bulk of Blackburn's poetry appeared originally in little magazines, many of them obscure and ephemeral; the collections in which a number of the poems reappeared were themselves mostly published by small presses, often in small print runs.

The arrangement of poems in this volume is chronological. The five divisions—1949–54, 1954–57, 1958–63, 1963–67, and 1967–71—represent, very roughly, periods of major change in Blackburn's style, locus—or both. In 1949, when the first poem in this book, "Cantar de Noit," was written, Blackburn was an "apprentice" poet at the University of Wisconsin; by 1954 he was coming into his own, writing assured, if still somewhat stylized, poems in New York City. In the spring of that same year, Blackburn went to Europe on a Fulbright Fellowship; the poetry he wrote in the three-and-a-half years spent in Spain and Provence is steeped in the atmosphere and rhythms of those places. Back in New York City from late 1957 through 1963, Blackburn wrote some of his most characteristic poetry, or at least that for which he is best known, particularly his series of subway poems. The next four years, those of his second marriage, saw a regrouping, sometimes a dissolution, of the work. In late 1967, on his return to Europe, Blackburn began writing new, more open poems, which he called "journals"; he continued experimenting with this form until his death in Cortland, New York, in 1971.

In making this selection, I've felt looking over my shoulder the many friends and admirers of Blackburn whom I came to know in the course of editing the *Collected Poems*. Certainly they, along with anthologists and earlier editors, tacitly influenced my decisions—but the only influence I consciously welcomed was that of Blackburn himself, always giving serious consideration to poems he included in his collections, submitted to anthologies, and performed frequently at readings.

E. J.

1949–54

CANTAR DE NOIT

This bird speaks to me from the night,
From chilled autumn dark;
There is plaint in the song he makes
In his midnight field.
He remembers a sun-shaft smile
And soft air,
As I remember in my heart and
With my flesh
A smile that made the sundrench
Seem less bright,

Made my soul more lucid than
Any sunlimned world.
And on my back, awake in a
Single bed,
This room without light, hearing
A bird speak
My flesh to me, I, groping
For the light switch,
Must climb out, struggle into
A robe, making
Two late singers mourning
A lost time.

THE BIRDS

I want them to come here
I want to see them here
 at this round boulder.
                    White spots against the sky, each
                    there, a swollen white spike on each
of the line of rotten piles that reach
                    out from shore.
Others skim the sea, strange
cries, wings flapping
                    I want to see them here
                    I want them to come here.
                    I swim my mind, swim it
in the moving water of all my world
          in moving clouds
                    in sun.

                    And I was young
and neck began to wobble clear, but feet
          were rooted in this beach, for I
feared the dark march to the sun again; and each
stiff inner motion moved me into song
                    instead of into living :
but now I know what thing is worth the having
and fear the imperfection in my singing; but now
can lie here and swim my mind in it
                    and still know when to leave
                    touch bottom to darkness where
I no longer fear to ask much of the gods.
          It has taken me a long time to realise
I want them to come here
I want to see them here.

SPRING

My branch cut from the tree I
spin towards ground
and the rain paints her human image on the earth
the amputation proving both costly and painful

Yet the rain
yet I spring with it

But we may not sin here, neither any repenting
and tho I spring with it
      I
           am ashamed of the naked impulse
           and ashamed of not sinning anyway

THE EYE OF THE STORM

Struck by the wind, the taut guitar of rain

moves panicked on my window, phrase and chord.

Speee-k to mee of love

      W I N D   R A I N ,   speak!

Lord, how my head cruises, wind!

no matter she has not come to me wet thru
that I might warm her and do for and to, but
speak of her wind, speak of love where
      she is all music stilled
and rich
and dark as a spring night.

      Till light comes
I sit here pretending to
warm myself with coffee, furious :

cake half-eaten, the bed turned down,
the dishes washed, I lower my head
hearing the long rain wash the city
hearing the wind bellow the streets
delirious with wetness, myself, gone
serious with storm, molten with fright—

      Over
her somewhere sleeping head the storm
      swings whose
eye is in this room,
and in tomorrow's sun no dissonant
splinter of night's tune   but she
smiling, will take my guitar from off the wall
and name a song she likes while I
complain, happy and warm as any singer in Spain.

COMMITTEE

      My two cats sit toward me resting,
one on the desk and one on the bookcase beside it:
half-open eyes like yellow flowers

             move at intervals from

my face to the door and back, asking
when my girl will open it, for she has missed the hour.
      When the key turns in the lock
they will be at the entrance before me
             rubbing her ankles.

Until that time I shall imitate their curious patience
          and rest here with half-closed eyes
          and hear the clock and my breathing.

THE RETURN

He had sought
sour badlands and walked
desert hills covered with flat stones,
year of the red-necked buzzard flying,
fox' bark:
muddy coloured snakes, lizards sunned
stretched under clear air on rock,

fled as he approached.

And the long-forgotten came upon him in that place
and thrills of love shook him in the dark;
but the desert wind that had touched his face
now grated a lesson like rattle of death

and the animals watched.

Thus the footmarks turned
and thru the burnt land he marched,
slowly, mountains came nearer,
foot-tracks thru the hills, then
roads: dust rising, an
occasional horseman
gazing from behind his eyes at the traveler.

As yet, no words.

At the turn of a hillside he saw a crowd
of steep roofs, flat roofs, stone spires, bridges,
towers, and from
the net of shaded streets, the unceasing
hum rose to him
and his love defined itself as need

to add himself.

He knew beforehand the brutal look in their faces
their coarse words, their clanging loud-mouthed crafts
        and his heart kept off:
but thru low windows the long tables at evening
                and the children
wriggling excitedly on old knees.

        The feast day and bells
         tuned minds to joy:
fiddles reeled thin thru streets
                dancing, dancing,
folk ran from their doorways laughing,
women shouted window to window, the town
blurred under his eyes
and his love pinched
and staggered his ankles down thru the warm dust
           to speech
           casting at dice to buy his loss.

DEATH AND THE SUMMER WOMAN

Curious reason in the choice of words:
        "Summer" I said, after my second thought,
        "Summer is all your flower. Much

harder or softer than you are
one could say Spring" and yes,
        the green arched
aching intensity you wear
fringes that season, but Summer
      is your sea-green innocence;
       is the brown easy

slope of back and shoulders moving into surf,
how you lower your head when I try to look at you,
a hot sunny innocence, yet sea-green coolness

and your eyes know us;
your open palms, the sweated tracings
show the door stands open.

                       But the trap of will
will trip it snap shut like brass
                       the slightest touch,
haul you hooked inside and kill the season, Death
               smiling cool at you the whispered

                                        "no"

THE LANNER

Delicately ravaged,
scared
afraid to lean into it;
tongue
swollen in my mouth, the
tune
caught in the throat.
Words,
the words, damn them
thrash in the ear
bash in the ear,
will, by no means,
move.

Nothing,
nothing remembered singly
but all
here
stumbling about singing
altogether too loud
and way off key.
Afraid
to sit back and let the song ride clear,
afraid it won't ride and won't ride clear.
This purpose dares not shape an imperfect bell.

But fumbling seizes purpose by the nape, and
together they roll and stagger toward the tune,
liquored up and blind to sleep it off,
dreaming Segovia, Lorca and Daniel.
                    And at 5 A.M.?

                    Dawn
falters from the horizon of the sea,
hesitates behind the skylight, filters
                    through
                    and I
rise straight up from the cot
rising from that metrical inferno, feel
the first notes break, sit down again, start
a low cadence riding articulate
in the grey light
                    and know that
                              again

the lanner is my bird.

One day she will move

straight up from the hand, and diving

prove herself my huntress, seize

the word, the line, the stanza, all

I hawk for ever:

another day

the bag hangs empty from my shoulder

because of this coward.

But the days when she is forward

when she is all there is of boldness,

I am glad she is my huntress,

and the lanner is my bird!

FOR MERCURY, PATRON OF THIEVES : A LAUREL

The hour before dawn
fog came in . Stayed all day .
Ragged thin filter of sun, a lover's
touch on bared skin .
Dock smell, oil, machinery
smell of sea,
pulse of city in thigh-vein,
sea-pulse distends the delicate vein in the temple,
throbbing above eyes still caked with night . The head
sways
bends in amphibious light
on the dangerous shoulders of the day.

At dawn
all places equal :
Athens, Paris, Brighton Beach and Arizona.
The trap.
The bear
dies in the trap : Mercury too a thief,
the cat's walk lives . The difference
is feet

Feet !   The cool air brushes an arm and
feet spring the walk, respond to the swaying head.
The sensitive pavement reacts, receives
holds the off-weight tread, holds and releases
wings to the god's foot man's foot, sends
an alternating current of love and sense
   between man and street.

Pay down the price of cigarettes, receive the pack, grasp
in the living hand, the cellophaned firmness . Dammit
   enjoy your smoke.
The sidewalks of spring
love us as we love them, no better, caress the feet
the way the feet press them . And sun, fog-
filtered, touches like lover   lovers' arms
who thieve each other   naked   tall   and warm.

THE SEARCH

I have been looking for this animal for three days now
   and four nights
   not finding him.
Probing into the corners of my mind to find him,
glancing at store windows and into the faces of women.

  Sometimes I think it is a bird
   but then again not.
  Once I was sure it was a lizard
facing my left trouser-leg at a pet-shop window,
   crouched
with his tongue darting out in primeval coldness.
But I found myself looking again the following day.

So neither very-hot blooded nor cold blooded,
   those early creations.
It is small, it has four legs and fur.

I saw it, almost, under the dark brows
of a Puerto Rican child in the street.
        A garment worker.
    Her belly was small and round
        and it was growing.
But she saw I looked and the thing changed in her eyes
        and it was a woman.
I have a woman. That's not what I look for now.

        My cat gave me a clue.
He was lying on his back, his feet in the air
        asleep.   The thing was
    the mixture of attitude in his face,
the sublime trust and disdain, careless, sure.

    Turned out it was a hamster.
You find them in cages with treadmills, which
        seems to me a symbol.
    This from a magazine someplace
        with a set of pictures.
    Mine was not in a treadmill. He
lay on a ledge in the sun in the window
    of a shoe-repair shop on Sixth Avenue,
his legs stretched out behind him, sideways,
for he lay on one side in the sun
washing his face with one paw like a cat
        ignoring the traffic.

        And having found him out
I didn't know what to make of him, except that
he was a small fat rodent and looked careless,
that he was a mammal and sure.

AFTER DINNER

The small cats disoblige to pose; she
lays pad and conte crayon on the ledge.

Lilt of conversation.   Then.

" H E Y !   Those are my art materials!"
The pointed living gesture turns to flight. The cats

work under cover of our conversation.

Nor is reading simple : a second one
presses affectionately against his sweater
                    effectively decomposing
                    the page suddenly
                    in mid-sentence.

              A third arrives to reinforce the fun.

Half-pleased to find it in his lap
"Jeezus Christ, another!"   and she,
"Leave my goddamned conte crayon alone!"

              The first resumes
eyeing the bookcase, a more ambitious scheme.

              They have the situation well in hand.

FRIENDS

Perhaps it is right
that you shall not be there. Perhaps
good friends should remain apart.

    the sea beats on the rocks
                or that proximity

But there are friends, also close in space.

THE CONTINUITY

The bricklayer tells the busdriver
and I have nothing to do but listen:

Th' holdup at the liquor-store, d'ja hear?
        a detective
watch't   'm for ten minutes
        He took it anyway
        Got away down Broadway   Yeah?
                    Yeah.

          And me:

      the one on the Circle?
              Yeah.
Yeah?   I was in there early tonight.

        The continuity.
     A dollar forty-
two that I spent on a bottle of wine
is now in a man's pocket going down Broadway.

Thus far the transmission is oral.

Then a cornerboy borrows my pencil
to keep track of his sale of newspapers.

THE MIRROR

The lazy dragon of steam issues
                  from manhole cover.   Tires hiss
The wet streets of my city speak to me

this rain
now almost stopped

                  or say :
even with winter rain here, youth is back
to walk on these reflections
but now the neon images shimmering
                      across cement are
more solid than glass or building block or stone
or
my image?

THE SUDDEN FEAR

The marble blocks guarding the gates to the park are monsters
wobbling, crushing in as we try to get in
                      past them

                  They are not always that way. Sometimes
a summer day, we stroll thru happy, not heeding them, into
a glistening day
                green grass   warm smells   all

                    But not tonite, not
now, at the beginning of winter   (how

                              white they are

                              how cold)
now, seen at side-glance from   the seat of a bus going
                        past and away from them

THE ASSISTANCE

On the farm it never mattered;
behind the barn, in any grass, against
any convenient tree,

                    the woodshed in winter, in a corner
if it came to that.

But in a city of eight million,   one
stands on the defensive.

                    In the West 59th St. parking lot
it has long since sunk into the cinders.

But in the shallow doorway of
a shop on Third Avenue, between

                    the dark and the streetlight,
it was the trail of the likewise drinking-man who preceded me
                    that gave me courage.

THE SUNLIT ROOM

Here

we find our private temporary limit
the depths we swim to and then
spring the gap
                              ourselves
what has been possible
for us strangely
from the beginning

THE DISSOLVING FABRIC

He who has own wound
cannot speak of it.
Nor is there any geography which
takes cognizance of it.

To know and then to heal
that is the rule.
But discipline is not sufficient
despite our speculations.

And there is no one, not the god
who understood it.
And the fact is that she withdrew it,
the fact is that she owned it.

She possessed her own life, and took it.

THE EVASION

The light that enters
not a definition

Against the light
your polite uncertainty keeps asking questions which
can be answered obliquely:
your innocence demands, almost, no definition,
edges us to those areas where no
syntax or other act can be direct

The other is a warm-hearted fool
and very likeable

Against your murmuring silence he puts
a graceful chatter,
disgracefully entertaining, entertains
his hangover, takes
what is his due, the stranger's gift
black bread and chowder, our hot spiced liquors
But you

eat and drink in silence . No one knows
what ghost you feed
Against his clumsy warmth you lay

                    (the light fading behind you

a distant politesse, an ambiguity
which does not answer our hospitality
                    tho it is you we greet .

1954–57

THE QUEST

No image
is decisive argument
                and it cuts me loose
                        altogether
                to feel, the roots set down
                stubbornly
                into rock, even
                strained by this.

CABRAS

To sing the democratic man today
or the marxist man, for that,
is no proposition.
So I sing goats.

Hardly anymore the issue, to
move to the line, take up the quarrel against it. Each
man is forced back some by the damned noise, will
hold any line against it, his own.

What else can be intelligent or warm—
no communal man at all.
Some little human conspiracy in letters
or the possible handshake,
but such accidents of fate or inner nature
are certainly occasional—yet

all of us eat and shit and walk or ride.
But goats, asses, pigs, sheep enjoy
equal rights,
make their droppings and stink, each
according to his natural inclination.

Burros came up the hill today with flagstones,
left their dung on the steps, were patient,
walked very carefully, without resentment.

Sheep die silently, pleading with their soft eyes,
pigs scream under the knife, and for a long while.

The goats in the next field, however, are hobbled,
being otherwise difficult to catch,
    they are so quick and stubborn
and full of fun.

THE FRIENDSHIP

Now we can wonder
how that star that

sat there
so high, so
high on the peak of the mountain

                (follow, the seasons follow

now appears
in a cleft between hills
further down, further down

      And the light appears dimmer
      at least it has more red in it

Now, too, we can wonder
that the truck moving through
the town below
casts more light

      (can, besides, make noises
      being in that sense humanistic
      i.e., a human contraption

tho
the shadows close in behind it

      Starlight casts no shadows
      Better not play with stars
      Better the shadow dissolving,
      better the human contraction

      So the light appears dimmer,
      so there is more red in it,
      so it does not sit so high, so
      cool on the peak of the mountain

It takes a man to drive the truck.
The shadows close in behind him.
And the seasons follow.

VENUS

This star, see,

she comes up and leaves

a track in the sea.

Whatcha gonna do, swim

down that track or

drown in the sea?

THE GIFT AND THE ENDING

The one-half moon is over the mountain
and the star is over the sea.
    The star will go down
    into the sea.
The moon will also go down.

And the cat sits on the rock
chewing the bacon rind I have given him.

He took it from my wife's hand,
still, she may not touch him.

Later he will clean his face,
lick himself in much contentment.

    The moon will also go down.

A PERMANENCE

The bear
does not go down into the sea.
He is also called the Chariot.
    There are not many things eternal.

He takes the fates of men in his paws,
strews them all over the horizon.

    Seven stars swinging forever.
He strews them all over the horizon.

He is there
even in the day, when we do not see him.
He does not ever go down
never, into the sea.

WNW

Rosy-fingered dawn
with her saffron cloak
spreads it over the world, and all that
but on this coast we see only sunsets.

One would have to swim a mile out into it,
the same sea,
or go in a boat
to see Himself rising over the headlands
or out of the ocean stream;
the mountains rise up from the sea-bord,
the angle of this coast.

THE STORM

The field below dark green, solid and
dark, filling us
with a sense of the ominous.
At the horizon, a line of cumulus
with black along its belly.

"See? There is light on the slopes!
It is only one cloud
darkening those fields."

"I know it is only one cloud.

But it is ominous.

Did you look at those on the horizon?"

"I looked at the horizon.

It might blow over."
                    "Yes

                    it might blow over."

**BAÑALBUFAR, A BRAZIER, RELATIVITY, CLOUD FORMATIONS &
THE KINDNESS & RELENTLESSNESS OF TIME, ALL SEEN THROUGH
A WINDOW WHILE KEEPING THE FEET WARM AT THE SAME TIME AS**

End of February

beginning of Lent.   How prevent

the clouds from moving now.   Where

                    sunlight falls . . .

        The walls

keep the wind out, but the house

                    cold, cold

Feet under the fold

        of the tablecover

edge toward the brazier under-

neath.   Old house.

Warmer outside, where is

        sun

                    when sun is.

        Sheaves of love and talk

        wave at the attention.

More hot coals are added.   Loud
thanks.
Focus on direction.   Analyze.
Keep the eyes
peeled
are changing now, clouds

Southwind:
and lines of clouds walk across the mountains, straight
across the sea;   the land, the mountains at angle.
Between the cloudbanks
sun falls.
Lemon trees
outside the window under sun
making a sweet quadrangle:
parallel lines of sun straight,
trees bent
under the double weight,
wind
fruit.
How prevent
the clouds from moving, now that sun . . . . Sunlight on

pear blossom, apple blossom, the red wall,
roofs' tile, red and yellow, yellow!
lemons under sun.
The mountain   now in one
shadow, huge;
the colors in old wood, the door, sun,
dark green of pines, dark blue of rock, more

cloud, the
wing of a cloud
passes.
Alas!
Alles, ala, the wing, everything
goes.

No.
Always is always all ways.
No, not so.
My love says to me, —Not so.
I am humble under this wind
but stupid, and hopeful even.

"Come
into this cold room.
The smell of wildflowers is
in every corner.
The mind
is filled with flower smell and sun
even when sun is not."

THE HOUR

Noon-and-a-half :

waiting to eat

we have sat on the stone bench in the sun for an hour

ignoring the time

except for the time of our bodies, our

hunger . We

sit here fixed,

driven back on ourselves,

                      listening,

caught in the blue silence of this wind,

    hungering for that too

                after northern winter

listening to the warm gnawing in the stomach,

    the warm wind

through the blossoms blowing .

THE MARGIN

Late morning on this island: cocks

enchanted with the sun

compete across the mountains,

blossoms here already in February!

Excitedly, we sit here talking

nonsense in this sunlight.

The lemon tree is heavy,

these giddy roosters also crow at noon

just to hear each other.

A few good things are left on earth

and they are not manufactured.

RUE DU TAUR

for Jean Séguy

THE MIRACLE HAS happened .

Here, after long winter, to see

this man

looking at his town,

walking thru the air of it,

tho the sun is still pale on the walls

but thru the air of spring

looking at the sun on the walls

smelling it

head high .

Not a glance at the window of the bookstore

which has taken   5   minutes of his attention

each time he has passed it

all winter .

Toulouse, March 1955

THE IDIOT

I do not stammer
but speak slowly
when I speak.

Having often nothing to say,
I say nothing.
Having often nothing to say
sometimes I talk too much.

But there are no rules :
and sometimes I am in
without great division between
intention and end.

But however I can be shrewd
I am hardly ever practical
and the matter rests unconcluded.

VERBENA

You can have it by being in it
you can have it by dancing and drinking
you can have it by being jostled by crowds
                or standing in the street yelling
                or standing and listening quietly :
                but in words it is not possible
to have it.

                There were

                fires in all the streets!
at every intersection, bonfires,
noise all night in the streets
                in the parks
carnivals
                & fireworks.

Dancing all the next afternoon
in the Plaza de San Jaime,
the bodies weaving like wheat
a whole plaza-full of movement :
and when the music rises, comes
        down harder on the beat at

the end of the *coblas*, a whole sea
leaping circling saulting bodies, the
     waves of the sea.

    Go ahead, lieutenant, photograph it.

          In the Junta del Puerto
          2 streets blocked off for dancing.
Not the delicate & precise steps of the *sardanas*
    in the Plaza, the ordered circles,
     circles within circles, here
the individual abandon of couples
the individual shyness of couples
  and the music from loudspeakers
  and boys walking off to the beach with their girls.
          Fiesta.
          Potato chips and *churros*.

          Impossible, impossible,
the life's too near the skin—now look,
  in the Junta del Puerto, fires.
They drink beer from the glass *porones*,
2 streets blocked off by dancers, the music
audible from the shore, surf juxtaposing.
          Bars
             open all nite,
          fires throughout the city.
The clack of the watchman's stick,
the formal and delicate dancing.

          In the calle de los Marineros
          a small girl in a white dress
          a small boy with a firecracker.

BARCELONA
23-24 de junio
1955

PLAZA REAL WITH PALMTREES

At seven in the summer evenings

they crowd the small stone benches

back to back

five and six to a bench;

young mothers

old men

workers on their way home stopping

off, their faces

poised in the tiredness and blankness

recouping

taking the evening coolness

five and six to a bench.

Children too young to walk,

on the knees of their mothers

make

seven and eight to a bench.

The older ones play immies

or chase each other

or pigeons.

Sun catches the roofs, one side

                  of the arcade;

the whole of the plaza in shadow between

seven and eight of an evening.

              The man with balloons

              rises above it almost

              his face deflated & quiet

                              blank

              emptied of the city

              as the city is emptied of air.

              The strings wrapped to his hand

              go up and do not move.

              He stands at the edge of the square

              not calling or watching at all.

                          The cart

              with candy has food for the pigeons . . .

                        A lull,

            a lull in the moving,

            a bay in the sea of this city

                into which drift

five and six to a bench

seven and eight to a bench

> Now
>
> the air moves the palmtrees,
>
> faces.
>
> All of it gentle

Barcelona . 27 . VI . 55

EL CAMINO VERDE

The green road lies this way.
I take the road of sand.

One way the sun burns hottest, no relief, the other
sun   (the same)   is filtered thru
leaves that cast obscene
beautiful patterns
on roads and walls . And

the wind blows all day.
Hot . sirocco, a chain
of hot wind rattles across
high over the mountains
rushes down from the peaks to the sea
laving men's bodies in the fields between
Days when
the serpent of wind plucks and twists the harp of the sun.

In the green road, pale
gray-green of olives, olive-wood twisted
under the burning wind, the wet
heat of an armpit,   but in the mouth

this other road. And the dry heat of the mouth is the pitiful
possibility
of finding a flower in the dust.   Sanity . See
there, the white
wing of a gull over blindness of water,
the blank black wing of a hawk over stretches of forest . Wish
to hold the mind clear in the dark honey of evening light, think
of a spring
in an orchard
in flower
the soft sun amid ruins, down there
the serpent
hidden among sweet-smelling herbs, down there
a small palm offers its leaves to the wind .
On the mountain, olive,
o, live wood,
its flawless curve hangs from the slope.

Hot . sirocco . covers everything
and everyone, all day, it blows all day as if
this were choice, as if
the earth were anything else but
what it is, a hell.   But
blind, bland, blend the flesh.
Mix the naked foot with the sand that caresses it, mix
with the rock that tears it,   enter
the hot world.

Cave of the winds .
What cave?   the

> reaches of Africa
> where an actual
> measure

> > exists.

THE LETTER

> The legs being uneven
> the chair opposite wobbles by itself .

Clear air of Adriatic morning
On the bridge the captain reads it out:

> 49 hrs.   14 min.   42 sec.

sextant error   02 min.   0 sec.

> 49 –   12 –   32,   he reads,
> 49 –   02 –   00

> > second correction . The

horizon a perfect circle .
Ship the moving center of the circle .

> The sun is the stick, an
> absolute time .

> Lat.   41° 34′ N
> Long.   16° 58′ E
> Declination of sun   24° 09′

Say I know where you are
Now you know where I am
Time on Board (not Greenwich)
9 hrs. 24 min. 52 sec.
the 3rd of August, 1955.

> Your son and daughter-in-law send you herewith
> greetings
> and that we thought of you,
> this, your day .

And there were dolphins this morning
early, tho I did not see them
and was reading .
Freddie told me about them .

> The barometer is rising .
> The sea is anyway fair
> *and* incredibly blue
> damned incredibly blue.

Horizon is a circle
and the ship its center
All sea-rings have centers, as we know,
and all worlds are one
> in appearance :
the rest a geometrical projection of
what otherwise might be proved a hell, but is
in fact an Eden, where no tree grows
and land is beyond imagining, my mother.
> The blue
> the blue .
> This is all my news.

Both of us are well and send our love

All things contain themselves and pass away

By this hand, the third day
of August . '55,
from the ARSIA
in a timeless sea .

NIGHT SONG FOR TWO MYSTICS

That man,
this man, never
satisfied
is almost enough.
The sense, the half-sense of his
of any man's in-
corruptible loneliness
incorrigible and terrified,
should be enough
to cave society in
his need and ours.

What's melancholy is the most abstract.
Yet skip it back
seven centuries,
that same centrifugal leaves a sediment
whose taste is sweet

'when the light from the beloved's room comes

        t o   i l l u m i n a t e

the chamber of the lover, then
all the shadows are thrown back,
then he is filled and surfilled
with his peculiar pleasures,
the heavy thoughts, the languors.
And the lover will throw all the furniture out of the room,
everything,
that it may contain his beloved'   That he may.

And Llull is taught what red is
'and what new vestments he shall put on,
what his arms are for
and what they shall embrace,
and how to lower his head to give the kiss'
which is good training for a lover.
But the beloved remains forever
far enough removed
and in a high place
as to be easily seen from a distance.
Which pride is unforgivable.

So you see where we stand, where you stood, Yeats?
And must it always lead to gods?
The man's shadow dissolves in shadows.
Most men go down to obliteration
with the homeliest of remembrances.

(pride, avarice, lust, anger
gluttony, envy & sloth

What are the positive virtues
which come between a man and his world,
estrange his friends, seduce his wife,
emasculate his god and general manager in charge of
blow his earth up?

(down, sailor,
blow the man

c o i l e d   d o w n   t h e r e

in the dark pools of the mind , their time

they wait the violent lunatic wind
at the star's dimming.

Dust, Yeats, all dust,
tho Llull remain a lover.

HOW TO GET THROUGH REALITY

The long low hills humped back against the night
filled with stars
Grey bursting nite-sprays of olive, miles of orchard
near the track

                                      Andromeda !

                 Orion !

The Car !

grey blossoms of olive trees
                the long hills

Those who work us, with   stones
who create us from our stone, who live
               among stones here
               the rest pass through
Our beauty under glass is your reality, unreachable
             sliding our gift to you

                                  Darkness

                pass through

Beauty is the daily renewal in the eyes of

Bursting sprays of olive
    the long hills
and behind them, stars

Stones,

staowns!

One could kick the glass out, no?

No.

Pass through.

RAMAS, DIVENDRES, DIUMENGA

Before the cathedral, the plaza

is a forest

tall fronds

The trunks are people in bright clothing

the plaza in bright sunlight

the yellow palm leaves waving

young forest on a brilliant breeze

in the bright air of heaven.

At no signal

the trees face the church

and stamp with the butt of the fronds

muffled sounds

but in unison.   Aediles

demanding for the whole people,   a benison

which is given.

Afterwards,

the children carry them mostly,

slowly through the streets of the city,

walking home from the mass.

"Mine is taller'n yours!"

—*El mío es mas alto qu'el tuyo!*

—*No es verdad! Mira! Mira!*

Whipped to competition, the palms wave unconcernedly

in the bright air

in the shadows.

Pigeons walk in the sunlight.

The people feed them.

o   o   o

Death day by the sea without crosses.   The beach

stretches its cold sands under

a dirty sky full of scud.   The wind

chill.

No trees, nothing to break it.

All the tears have fallen already into the sea.

Even the sourness of salt on the air is galling,

the surf   dull and lifeless   but continuing.

Clouds darken on the horizon at three o'clock.

The wind picks up.

o   o   o   o   o

The ark of the tabernacles

is drawn up by two white bullocks

with olive-branch tied to their horns.

They stand white and imperturbable

among the fireworks.

Barcelona . Sète . Firenze
Holy Week . 1956

SONG FOR A COOL DEPARTURE

When the track rises
the wires sink to the fields

Trees absorb them in and blot them out
black running
pencil-lines against the fields' green

Shrubbery close to the track goes by so
        fast it hurts the eyes

Rain has quit
We have arrived
at Salut or Castelnaudary

        A woman laughs harshly in the corridor
        The soldiers on either side sleep beautifully
peacefully, one with his mouth open, the
        other has his closed

The world is certainly diverse!
                    Wires begin again to
                    fall and rise
Small fruit trees stand in quadrangles
in a field otherwise planted
The brook tries to escape notice and where
                    shall I put 2
cypresses,
3 elms?

    Old woman in the corner
wrestles her rented pillows and cannot sleep
    One finally arranges itself
under her right arm, the other
entirely out of control, she clutches
on her lap, the comfortable weight,
her rented buffers against a hard world
and stares direct in front of her and cannot sleep

        My wife holds her face up for a kiss
        Brow puckered and tired, she also cannot quite
        sleep,
        worrying about a pair of sunglasses we
        left at someone's house yesterday
                    in the round of farewells.

        Having left that town
        we have left nothing behind.

The world is surely diverse enough
and if the information is sound, one
could ride forever and never fall off
            let others sleep—
I am so wide-awake I want to sing, while
the wheels turn, the windows clatter, the door
            jogs, the wires
rise and change and fall
and the green grass grows all round, all round
and the green grass grows all round . . . .

THE PROBLEM

My wife broke a dollar-tube of perfume

The arab

who owns the perfume shop insisted

    it was good luck

        Sure it was .

To break any vessel is, if we know

the appropriate formula to make it sacrifice

and know a god

to dedicate it to .

SIGNALS I. : TANGER, AUGUST 1956

1.   Even in Algeciras
        that cesspool :

when the wind came up suddenly
        on a hot afternoon,
a half-dozen people on that corner
scrambled
    to pick up
      gently
the empty cones of the ice-cream vendor
the gust had scattered .

2.

Tonite,

after   10   minutes watching

and listening to early roosters

a dog joining in from the street

          a lonesome ass

screaming from the market

for company

or food

     one

          burst toward the Spanish coast

          It was orange

THE NEEDLE

     Two blocks away

      night traffic goes whipping through

the avenue,

the fast motors.

It's not as tho one could see it

It's not as tho nothing were good

Even above the rooftops stars are mixed with cloud

      only the brightest come through:

the absolute bureaucracy of size and closeness

      which coefficient is power.

     But the cat

crosses the tiled roof at this hour

      in the dark night

      in the moon.

Málaga, Sept. 1956

MOSCA

A fly

sits &

scrubs his front feet,

then rubs his back feet together

cleaning them, then

washes his wings and his eye   .   Why

do people call flies dirty?

It looks like a pleasant process .

Self-absorbed & self-contained,

directed, especially in flight,

certainly curious and active—

W h y   i s   b u z z i n g   c o n s i d e r e d   i d l e ?

SUERTE

You shall not always sit in sunlight watching

weeds grow out of the drainpipes

or burros and shadows of burros

come up the street bringing sand

the first one of the line with a

bell

always.

With a bell.

Grace is set

a term of less than a year.

Another bell sounds the hours of your sun

limits

sounding below human voices,

counts the hours of weeds, rain, darkness, all

with a bell.

The first one with a bell always.

PAISÁJE

for Lorca

The mule walks on the sand
the man sits on the mule
The man's head sits on his shoulders
In his head

his eyes

look out

Five men are hauling a net
Gulls stroll at the surf's edge

the boats

on the sea
He looks between his mule's ears
at driftwood
at the birds
at sunglare
on the sea
off where day comes up

The mule leaves tracks on the sand
The man sits on the mule
His thoughts enter the air
His hands rest on his thighs
His eyes
        leave tracks on the wind

WHEE!

A goat lies in the grass beside

      a dry irrigation ditch

      Sun-glitter on sea
The boats drift in with the tide

Grazing cattle shy away

their long horns down & waving

In the hills the earth is red

    What a day!

Along the road, a gypsy

raises her water gourd

    in a fine

gesture to the passing bus

"QUIERES?"

      "PROVECHE!"

Nov 1956
Málaga-Algeciras

THE LOTTERY

Que buen
          números me quedan!

Mañana
          luck is
          always for tomorrow
          or tonight, when
the lottery is drawn

The horse-drawn carriage rattles
and clatters down the street
The horse's bells jingle
on the embroidered harness
The driver sits alert and wears
          a hat
               That is part of it

No one pays attention
The man will pay the driver
The cobbles will stay in the street
          but luck is felt
in the small dark stores, the doorways
as the sound of bells and hoofs
on cobbles

Travelers are good luck
here
they cry   *"maleta! maleta!"*
and run and touch the suitcase
          for luck

" Nail
those long shadows to my cross ! "
darkened doorways in sun-glare
a hammer
               Silence of black skirts
               unbelted
In the shadowed eyes
an ultimate patience
Death lives among the people
               as Life does

Luck never
Luck is for people in carriages
       for voyagers

Que buen números me quedan

         para H O Y !
     último par ' H O Y !

Nº 900549

Lotería Nacional

Sorteo
15 de Enero de 1957

El Portador
interesa 1 peseta al
número

59.174

MÁLAGA

Warm autumn night, light
    cloud, a few stars
Two young men run down the street
The sound of heels is normal
    like fiesta   almost

Pushcart on the corner
stopped roasting chestnuts early
    tonight   no one buying
Street conversations lasted
till long after midnight   Something
    going forever gone and again
        renewed

Even the quiet man next door
came home drunk and whistling

Sound of bicycle bells
& starting motor bikes
intermittent

Finally
the neighborhood
flickers and goes out   The
street lamp on the corner is
sentinel over the darkness

I have drunk my white wine and worked
I have lasted it out into silence

Smoke a cigarette on the balcony
Fine.   Light cloud, a few stars,
and the silence
World wheels its night and is warm
and empty
Everything in this underworld is asleep
or broken
A great white dog of silence lounges
alone there in the street
ranges curb to final curb
lies down under the street lamp
attentive
silent

Then a motor bike starts up
and a bicycle bell rings

LIGHT

White flare of stone in the sun
Day's begun   The sea
flickers the light back pleasantly

Last flare of red on white wall
Sun fall   into the sea
Night thickens gradually

Day's done   Stars come out
My thought   drifts like the sea
No grip between it and my act
I lose my luck too quickly

Cold   flare on the sea
Moon has come over the hill
Still no act by which I can
say there's been a man
in the house all day

Star on sea leaves a track
Act is something one does if
one thinks of it   And the cliff
falls away up   back of me
as the sea flashes up in the night
to touch and darken my sea

CAFÉ AT NIGHT

White snow of paper sugar
wrappers on the floor
next the counter.
2   men stand over their wine

               (white)

The men are white
The wine is white
          Two
women come in, they order hot

milk . Everything is still white

               (white)

Finally someone orders a cake
             I pluck
     courage up
     and order
            black
            coffee

               (black)

               Málaga, Winter 1956-57

               Un sirventes ai fach
               Contra'l ciutat de Tolosa
SIRVENTES   *On m'avia pretz ostalatge*
               D'un sen salvatge e famosa
               Del mons...

               PB / 1956

I have made a sirventes against the city of Toulouse
          and it cost me plenty garlic :
and if I have a brother, say, or a cousin, or a 2nd cousin,
I'll tell him to stay out too.
          As for me, Henri,

I'd rather be in España
pegging pernod thru a pajita
or yagrelling a luk
jedamput en Jugoslavije,
jowels wide & yowels not
permitted to emerge——
or even
in emergency
slopping slivovitsa thru
the brlog in the luk.
I mean I'm not particular,
but to be
in the Midi

now that rain is here,
to be sitting in Toulouse
    for another year,
the slop tapping in the court
to stop typing just at ten
 and the wet-rot setting in
and the price is always plus,
    I mean, please,
        must I?

Whole damn year teaching
trifles to these trout with trousers
tramping thru the damp
with gout up to my gut
taking all the guff, sweet
            jesus crypt,
        god of the he
brews, she blows, it bawls, & Boses
(by doze is stuffed)
by the balls of the livid saviour, lead be
back hindu eegypt-la-aad
before I'b canned for indisciblidnary reasons.

O god.
The hallowed halls
the ivy covered walls
the fishwife calls
& the rain falls

    Basta!

Jove, god of tourists, the whores in Barcelona are beautiful,
you would understand.
Weren't there Europa and Io? and Aegina, twin sister of Thebe
both daughters of Asopus?
and Maia and Antiope and
Niobe of the Thebans.
Eagle, ant, bull, beaver, flame, otter, how *not?*
Remember Leda?
I swan, you never felt old.
Your shower of rain at least was a shower of gold.
A gentle white bull with dewlaps.
The bulls in Barcelona are beautiful, Jove,
need no persuasion, are themselves as brave.

My old Guillem, who once stole this town,
thinking your wife's name enuf reason to . . .

St. Julian, patron of travellers, *mi des mercey* !

Who else invoke? Who else to save
a damned poet impaled by a *betterave?*
Mercury! Post of Heaven, you old thief, deliver me
from this ravel-streeted, louse-ridden, down-river-
gutter-sniping, rent-gouging, hard-hearted,
complacent provincial town,
where they have forgotten all that made this country the
belly of courage, the body of beauty, the hands of heresy,
the legs of the individual spirit, the heart of song!

That mad Vidal would spit on it,
that I as his maddened double
do —— too
changed, too changed, o
deranged master of song,
master of the viol and the lute
master of those sounds,
I join you in public madness,
in the street I piss
on French politesse
that has wracked all passion from the sound of speech.
A leech that sucks the blood is less a lesion. Speech!
this imposed imposing imported courtliness,   that
the more you hear it the more it's meaningless
& without feeling.

The peel is off the grape
and there's not much left
and what is left is soured
if clean :
if I go off my beam, some
small vengeance would be sweet,
something definite and neat,
           say total destruction.

Jove, father, cast your bolts
& down these bourgeois dolts !

    Raise a wave, a glaive of light, Poseidon,
    inundate this fish-bait !

       Hermes, keep my song
       from the dull rhythms of rain.

          Apollo, hurl your darts,
          cleanse these abysmal farts
         ·out from this dripping cave
          in the name of Love.

AFFINITIES I.

Montalban, N° 3, piso 2°
               is not exactly a pension
but a lady who rents rooms
               occasionally.

               And this big room has a small sink
               with a tap where
               no water has ever run:
                        and a drain
               in which one sets a cork.
               And on the brass plate is written

                  VERDAGUER   BARCELONA

that half-mad priest and poet
who listed all the peaks
in the catalunyan Pyrenees,
and here you are on a sink-drain.
Has it come to this, Jacint?

    Also,
there are two balconies looking out
over the roofs of the city
                    to the mountains.
And the lady, when she was younger,
                    lived in Granada
and remembers that García Lorca
always wore broad-brimmed Córdoban hats
        and a black string-tie, and was
                un chico simpático.

    So
it is not very strange
that the words are always there
when one looks out of the window
over the roofs of the city

    "and to see clouds and mountains
    in the motionless distances
    the heart twists in itself"

                "y al mirar nubes y montes
                en las yertas lejanías
                se quiebra su corazón
                de azúcar y yerbaluisa"

THE MISUNDERSTANDING

Morning sun clear on the mountain
            milky to seaward;
light cloud on the sea,
        where the boats ride, a *niebla.*
        Sun burning it off.
Light breeze from seaward.

From the far boats it looks as if
the cloud were over the island;
the blue mountains look milky.
Sun burning it off

l u m i n i s   c l a r i t a s

The day will resolve as crystal.
Light refracted through drops of perspiration
on a man's forehead
as he lifts his head from work
to speak.

CANCIÓN DE LAS HORMIGAS

Today makes   20   days
that some ants follow the same route
across   2   of these steps
never varying from the line.
Always this same line of ants
across the same   2   steps .
They may even be the same ants,
tho this would make a difference :
if the line budged one centimeter
it would make a difference.

And I do not know what the job is
or when it will be finished.

AT THE CROSSROAD

Close
but far

strayed into the half-cultivated country
        of meditation
woven into it wholly
enlaced in the rare herbs of silence

another,
a lost stranger, our friend
asleep, perhaps nearly dead

Nite-stir of silence
Water runs beyond summer its gutters
        Rustle of wind, light
        Moonlight over it all

In the next field
the May ass screaming
drunk on the new hay

DEPTH PERCEPTIONS

Man's hand touches the strings of his guitar
and the melody that emerges hammers
delicately
into this mound of night

                Oblong of brightness stands
                isolated in the mountain in
                a flat blackness
                without distances
                Someone has left a door open
                where there is no house

Truck labors up mountain
Crickets   night bird

                    Birdsong
          knifes the night open
          'Mound of night
          Tree of stars'
          Guitar hammers   will
lay all of it wide open—
fruit of tree and flower of tree
          burst with the seed
               of song!

                    Wrong.
The *guardia* turns up his radio and
it flattens, blares flat this rounded

     world of night

ATARDECER

The waves come in from the north

                         but softly

after   2   days of storm.
The wind comes in from the west

                         but gently

cross-hatching the pattern

                         Further out
               strips and circles
where the wind makes it otherwise
South to north in the strips

                         Dead
                         calm in the circles

Magic circles
that no wind
touches

Woman comes up the hill

                         but slowly

after   12   hours of work

after   2   hours of *camino* :

                rising before the light

                returning at sundown

She is over   60   years old, she don't

stop to admire the sunset

                Bandana is tight on the forehead

                Her stick is slow on the steps

1958–62

EL DÍA VIENE COMO UNA PROMESA DE CALOR

White clean sun in this dry street
from the white walls of white houses

Light of a half-cool morning with that dull
edge of heat
threatening us
with noon
            Our own hot swelter   But

for this one hour the sun cuts without
        glare, cleanly

Hoofs falter on the cobbles, goats
distracted by a tuft of grass between the low cobbles
quickened by the whirr of a switch in a boy's hand
on the inclined slope clatter   A shout

                The blue
of a slim   shimmering   boat-sustaining
                      sea
             Its slack sails

Close our eyes under these leaves
Breathe sweetly as tho we were wind
        moving these leaves
               black
beauty of such heat behind the eyes
             The leaves
             move by themselves   69

and cease

Each one his own hand
the cooled wine in the glass
touch lips of glass in the shadow

O C Y C L A D E S !

OKay .
Say another summer never come,
this would be enuf to die within .
a season where we wear our only skin
and beauty is what we daily are
in the presence of

LOVE SONG

Beauty is a promise of happiness

wa-hoo.

And happiness is a big, fat-assed

stuffed bird

that cannot, in its ideal state, move

off its fat

i.e., I am not Ariel,

I am Caliban,

and sometimes it is very ugly.

GOOD MORNING, LOVE!

Rise at 7:15

study the

artifacts

(2 books
1 photo
1 gouache sketch
2 unclean socks

perform the neces-

sary ablutions

        hands
    face, feet
    crotch

even answer the door

with good grace, even

if it's the light-and-gas man

announcing himself as " E D I S O N !

Readjer meter, mister?"

For Chrissake yes

    read my meter

        Nothing can alter the euphoria

The blister is still on one finger

    There just are

some mornings worth getting up

& making a cup

of coffee,

        that's all

HOMAGE TO THE SPIRIT

T H E   M O O N is my beloved
and I am Hercules
            holding it all

circle . circle . circle

Here, plant trees
in the proper
                (time
circle

There are   (there will be)   figs,
pomegranates, vines, the
                milk & the
honey—he said
& we shall come to judge the quick
                & the dead .   or

"move on the face of the waters"
that's for sure—
he said,
who is your comforter

**VENUS, THE LARK FLIES SINGING UP
BLUE SMOKE   BLUE GULL   THE
YEAR HAS COME FULL CIRCLE**

SUMMER had 5 . leafy center of the year

Winter was the three-headed bitch of Death
        Queen of the hive
        tomb of every hope

Clear is the color of wind, but it
        turns mad in March like any hare
        brained poet or golden thing

13 snipe on the sand beach
Wind blows off the cold sea
racing wild over foaming water

Death is twice on the ear-finger
Tree of Ross on the eve of the winter solstice
Here is the king's coffin and his cradle
The wheel
of existence has come full circle

The fire-garnet of Judah, terrible crystal
Saturday's child is a lonesome gull
crying over quiet waters
where the fish do not come
An alder-whistle will call the wind

Elder December's tree, also for hanging
and the power of witches
Its flowers are best at midsummer
at which time also, Death is . Maera . Deino
The 13th month begins one day
after my birth
Rook cries for the year that dies
Blood red
are the ragged leaves of the elder

Autumn goddess of rut and combat
the stags' horns' clash sounds on the wind

The oak door looks forward and backward, outward and inward
St. John is the day of our burning
Verbena is the odor of our burning . sweet
smell of scorched flesh . holocausts

in all the streets . fires
at all the crossroads . Death
at midsummer, making
magic at the top of hills
surrounding the city
Burned stumps of trees in the shovel .   The king
is dead! Long live the king!
burnt

Gayety? O yes, drink the unmixed wine and rejoice, but
rejoice in the blue haze on the hills
Blue is the smoke of burning weeds
Blue the skies before November rain
The swan is mute
The year comes down

REMAINS OF AN AFTERNOON

Flick of perfume, slight, and faintly bitter
on my wrist, where her hand had rested

Two wrist-bones and the soft thud of veins
printed on the hard flesh of her palm

The drinks
finished but untasted

THE FRANKLIN AVENUE LINE

at Park Place

or Dean Street

   across

decaying open platforms with their whitened wood

          wash

waves of weathered greenness down the line

waves of somewhere unimaginable blossoms blowing

a late spring to tired faces   in this half-

   forgotten slow half-empty train

passing in the rain   in slow dreams of pleasure

        toward the spur's end where

vaguely   in-

decisively   train and rain

come at the same

time

   to a measured

        stop

BROOKLYN NARCISSUS

        Straight rye whiskey, 100 proof
        you need a better friend?
        Yes.   Myself.

The lights
the lights
the lonely   lovely   fucking   lights
and the bridge on a rainy Tuesday night
Blue/green double-stars   the line
that is the drive and on the dark alive
gleaming river
Xmas trees of tugs scream and struggle

     Midnite

Drops on the train window wobble . stream
          My trouble
               is
it is her fate to never learn to make
             anything grow
        be born or stay
Harbor beginnings and that other gleam . The train
is full of long/way/home and holding lovers whose
     flesh I would exchange for mine
     The rain, R.F.,

     sweeps the river as the bridges sweep
     Nemesis is thumping down the line
     But I have premises to keep
     & local stops before I sleep
     & local stops before I sleep

           The cree-
           ping train
           joggles
           rocks across
           I hear
the waves below lap against the piles, a pier
           from which ships go
           to Mexico

a sign which reads

PACE O MIO DIO

     oil

           "The flowers died when you went away"

Manhattan Bridge
a bridge between
we state, one life and the next, we state
is better so
is no
      backwater, flows
           between us is
our span our bridge our
naked eyes
open here
see
bridging whatever impossibility. . .PACE!

PACE O MIO DIO

    oil

              "The flowers died. . ."
              Of course they did

Not that I was a green thing in the house

      I was once.
      No matter.

The clatter of cars over the span, the track
          the spur
the rusty dead/pan ends of space
    of grease

We enter the tunnel.

The dirty window gives me back my face

CLICKETY-CLACK

(for Lawrence Ferlinghetti)

                    I took
                    a coney island of the mind
to the coney
island of the flesh
                    the brighton local
riding
past church avenue, beverly, cortelyou, past
                    avenues h & j
king's highway, neck road, sheepshead bay,
brighton, all the way to stillwell
avenue
            that hotbed of assignation
            clickety-clack

I had started reading when I got on
and somewhere down past newkirk reached
number   29   and read aloud
                    The crowd
in the train
looked startled at first but settled down
to enjoy the bit
even if they did think I
was insane or something
and when I reached the line : " the cock
of flesh at last cries out and has his glory
                    moment God "
some girl sitting opposite me with golden hair
fresh from the bottle began to stare dis-
approvingly and wiggle as tho she had ants
somewhere where it counted
                    And sorry to say
5   lines later the poem finished   and I
started to laugh like hell   Aware
of the dirty look I was getting I
stared back at her thighs imagining
what she had inside those toreador pants besides
                    her bathing suit and, well
                    we both got off at stillwell

Watching her high backside sway and swish down that
street of tattoo artists, franks   12   inches long, past
                    the wax museum and a soft-drink
                    stand with its white inside,

I stepped beside her and said: " Let's
fling that old garment of repentance, baby ! "
                    smitten, I
hadn't noticed her   2   brothers were behind me

                    clickety-clack

                    Horseman, pass by

THE ONCE-OVER

The tanned blond
                    in the green print sack
in the center of the subway car
                                        standing
tho there are seats
                    has had it from
1 teen-age hood
1 lesbian
1 envious housewife
4 men over fifty
(& myself),   in short
                    the contents of this half of the car

                    Our notations are :
long legs, long waist, high breasts (no bra), long
neck, the model slump
                    the handbag drape & how the skirt
cuts in under a very handsome
                                        set of cheeks
'stirring dull roots with spring rain'   sayeth the preacher

        Only a stolid young man
    with a blue business suit and the New York Times
    does not know he is being assaulted

So.
She has us and we her
all the way to downtown Brooklyn
Over the tunnel and through the bridge
                    to DeKalb Avenue we go
all very chummy

She stares at the number over the door
                    and gives no sign
Yet the sign is on her

AT&T HAS MY DIME

After your voice's frozen anger

emptied the air between us, the

silence of electrical connections

the vacant window pale, the

connection broken ::

                    breaks in now

empty bravado of bar conversation, some

lonesome truck shifting gears

uptown on the avenue . Winter

has come much closer

Buy myself an ale

Manage to get it down

somehow .

THE ROUTINE

Each day I open the cupboard
& the green shoots of my last onion
have in the dark grown higher

    A perverse & fairly final pleasure
that I love to watch him stretching himself
secretly, green sprouting shamelessly in
this winter, making a park in my kitchen, making
spring for a moment in my kitchen

that, instead of eating him
    I have watched him grow

ETRUSCAN TOMB

Leer

and that spine moved

back against another (not surprising)   extension

of time(?)less stone is time perceived.

Let

the bereaved laugh with remembrance : here

one hand cups the handsome uppermost breast,

the other, the cup itself! A feast is death!

Across a slab of centuries, the living

flesh need not doubt itself or what they meant.

The slow brown eye of time and the quick blue

eye of lust

have crossed the line, forgiven themselves, become

an ornament.

MEDITATION ON THE BMT

Here, at the beginning of the new season
before the new leaves burgeon,   on
either side of the Eastern Parkway station
               near the Botanical Gardens
they burn trash on the embankments, laying
barer than ever our sad, civilised refuse.

1   coffee can without a lid
1   empty pint of White Star, the label
               faded by rain
1   empty beer-can
2   empty Schenley bottles
1   empty condom, seen from
1   nearly empty train
               empty

               empty

               empty
Repeated often enough, even the word looks funny.

Man in an alley carrying a morning load already
               walks
only by propping his hand against a thick red
               line
painted on a building wall,   while he goes past
coffee-can   beer-can   condom   bottles & fire
               past
faded brick and pock-marked cement to somewhere
relieve his bladder in the sorrow of a sun-shot morning

with some semblance of privacy, some-
how needed here . Cold . Sad

winter morning in spring where it is cold while
this man is high and the sun is high and there are no
rules governing the award of prizes to the dead.

My eyes

enter poor backyards, backyards

O I love you

backyards, I make you my own, and you
my barren, littered embankments, now that you
've a bit of fire to warm & cleanse you, be
grateful that men still tend you, still will
rake your strange leaves
your strange leavings.

Poor Brooklyn soil
poor american earth
poor sickening houses
poor hurricanes of streets, both
your subterranean and your public lives go on
anyhow,   beneath
refuse that is a refusal, with alienated, uneasy, un-
reflective citizens, who will be less un-
happy, more contented and vacant, if they
relieve their bladders against some
crappy wall or other.

HOT AFTERNOONS HAVE BEEN IN WEST 15TH STREET

Here, in late spring, the summer is on us already
                  Clouds and sun,
        a haze over the city.   Outside my
window the ailanthus nods sleepily under
                    a hot wind, under
           wetness in the air, the brightness
of day even with overcast.   The chair on the next roof
           sits by itself and waits
for someone to come stretch his length in it.   Suddenly

thunder cracks to the south over the ocean, one can
                 shuteye see
the waves' grey wife, the storm, implacably stride
rain nipplings on the surface of the sea, the waves
            powerfully starting to rise, raise their
                  powers before the hot wind
The endless stretchout to Europe disappears, the
rainsweep moving toward the city rising caught in the haze-hot
                island atmosphere
           Hate anger powers whip toward the towers rising
from the hum of slugbedded traffic clogging avenues, the trees
           of heaven gracing their backyards crazily
           waving under the strengthening wind

                 sun brighter
                 more thunder
                 birdsong
                 rises shrilly announcing

the storm in advance in encroach in abstruse syllables of pure
SOUND . SONG . SOMEONE
comes to the porched roof to cover the chair from the thunderfilled
wet atmosphere,   there is
nothing clearly defined wrong I can see except
I must go uptown and see what other storms there
be, there

And paint the inside of my wife's white filing cabinet red
that all things may be resolved   correct   and dead   .

CITY SUNSET

Pink and blue.

The pink striations angle down the sky

enter the southern deeps,   keep

laying out across my eye

asleep where it may not lie down

tell lies truly

and see

love's breasts at attention, at rest, at

my hand, orange

sand,   this

sunset you also see

but with two islands between you and me—

And if the sun is down

        our hearts

     the lights, the darks

they still are up, are high   o

dance with me

     O,

        dance

           with me !

THE PURSE-SEINE

Fierce luster of sun on sea, the gulls
           swinging by,
      gulls flung by wind
aloft, hung clear and still before the
          pivot
    turn
        glide out
riding the wind as tho it were
         the conditions of civilisation

But they are hungry too,
and what they do that looks so beautiful, is
    hunt .

The side of your face so soft, down, their cried falls, bitter
broken-wing graces crying freedom, crying carrion, and
we cannot look one another in the eye,
        that frightens, easier to face

the carapace of monster crabs along the beach . The empty

shell of death was always easier to gaze upon

than to look into the eyes of the beautiful killer . Never

    look a gull in the eye

Fit the 300-pound tom over the pursing lines, start it sliding
down the rope to close the open circle, bottom of the net, weight
thudding down thru the sea

brass rings hung from the lead line come closer together, the tom
pushing the rings ahead of it, the purse line drawing thru them,
taking up the slack, the school sounding the fish streaking by
toward that narrowing circle
    and out . . .

Waiting behind the skiff, birds sit on the sea, staring off, patient

   for what we throw them . We

   merely fight it, surf, and that other day. No

bed ever was until this, your face half-smiling down your swell of half-

sleep, eyes closed so tightly they will admit

   nothing but fear and stars . How can we

call all this our own? and shall we dare? admit the moon? full

bars of song from nightbirds, doors of the mind agape and swelling?

   Dream again

that orange slope of sand, we belting down it hand upon hand, the birds

    cry overhead

the sea

lies in its own black anonymity and we here on this bed

enact the tides, the swells, your hips rising toward me,

    waves break over the shoals, the

sea bird hits the mast in the dark and falls

with a cry to the deck and flutters off . Panic spreads, the

    night is long, no

  one sleeps, the net

is tight
we are caught or not, the tom sliding down ponderous
                    shall we make it?
                    The purse closes.

The beach is a playground . unsatisfactory, but we
pretending still it's play swim out too far, and reaching
back, the arms strain inward
Waters here are brown with sand, the land too close,
                    too close, we drown
                    in sight of
I love you and you love me . . .

RITUAL VI.

Grids and lines

keep all our melting time

                    •

        the roof dissolves under the sun

        a map melting and changing like Africa

        only it is snow and the continents shift

A shimmer hardly to be shook off

assails the birds as the birds assail the air

with their complaints

        Plants spread

their leaves in the sun

while in the sun snow

slides from the roofs, icicles crash,

blup-drip of icicle together with

sudden sparrowsong

burst at the sun thaw Sunday, keep

measure of our love

And here you sit in the sun with something

sunday about the newspaper and coffee, the egg

leavings drying in the cup, and your new

haircut, the face so soft, the sweet line of

mouth, smoke rising, cigarette

                  moving with the hand

                  table to a mouth and down

my fingers reach and trace the loving line it

                  makes at me, a mouth

laughing . . .

    Who is this madman

who wishes for a subdued life of leisurely gestures?

7TH GAME : 1960 SERIES

—for Joel—

Nice day,
sweet October afternoon
Men walk the sun-shot avenues,
                    Second, Third, eyes
                    intent elsewhere
ears communing with transistors in shirt pockets
                    Bars are full, quiet,
discussion during commercials
                    only
Pirates lead New York 4-1, top of the 6th, 2
Yankees on base,   1 man out

What a nice day for all this !
Handsome women, even
dreamy jailbait, walk
                    nearly neglected :
men's eyes are blank
their thoughts are all in Pittsburgh

Last half of the 9th, the score tied 9-all,
Mazeroski leads off for the Pirates
The 2nd pitch he simply, sweetly
                    CRACK!
belts it clean over the left-field wall

Blocks of afternoon
acres of afternoon
Pennsylvania Turnpikes of afternoon . One
                    diamond stretches out in the sun
                    the 3rd base line

and what men come down

it

The final score, 10-9

Yanquis, come home

RITUAL IV.

Seedlings

a season old

lemon trees, orange, lime, their leaves

     differing shades of green, differing

green shadows in dumb sunlight streaming beautiful

past their pots and boxes, sill to red wall, to white,

     beams holding their dust motes

     Saturday A.M.,   juice and coffee

     bacon and eggs and peace

     in a fresh-painted room

You sit here smiling at

me and the young plants . This

paper is covered with coffee-cup and bacon stains

        The dust motes

        float . Everything

grows,

and rests

WORKING LATE ON A HOT NIGHT

It says quarter-to-6 on one watch

and 3 A.M. on another

and the spots on the floor of my livingroom are

                from where the ice-cubes melted

But not everything is that

predictable

and the baskets of bread at an Italian bakery's cellar

                round the corner were

                moons or unloved

loves, things we never eat, but still

hot.   I went down and touched one.

MARINE CUMULUS : THE VALUE OF THE SYSTEM

        The wind moves them

        as tho there were something else

            she had forgot to do

        Towering mountains of cloud step over the city

        marching toward the Atlantic . dream

            of sunlight on them

The typist's clatter has hummed along all afternoon

some song behind the teeth

eyes the window obliquely

watching the clouds swim over Queens

heading toward the Atlantic . adjusts

      her typing table

      and the chair

dream of sunlight on them

facing the window, not

watching the keys

RITUAL I.

> "The fiesta does not celebrate
> an event, it
> reenacts it"
> *In this way time emerges* .

Procession with candles around the streets of that town :

hands raised and cupped to shield the tiny flames

        a timeless gesture

        as that slow walk

        is

from church along the main street to the second store

            then turn

            left, downslope

      to the lower street sinking past

      Ca'n Font, down

      past the lower line of houses .

Street rising gently to the road, back past

café

tailor's house

      the stairs

           the stores

                  dark suits and white shirts

the line of men, dark

dresses, dark shawls, veils, the line of

women's heads down   .   watching their own feet moving

        slowly   .   slowly   .   A-
                        ve, a-ve,
                        Ave Ma-ri-a,

                        A-ve, a-ve,
                        Ave Ma-ri-a

The touching directness of one lady tourist

who joined the procession

end of the women's line   .   suddenly

the angular figure in a traveling suit

        instead of a rosary, carried

        a white pocketbook   .   stood out

A german anthropologist lady who must have known

                what an

anomaly she appeared, and could not care, except to

add her poor self at the end of the line

Reaving my lady
half-asleep
in the dawn light

       Meat every Thursday
       when the calf
       is killed

              Mail from the bus at 4:30
              fresh milk at   5

The german lady with her white pocketbook .

End of a timeless act of the peoples of earth .

PARK POEM

From the first shock of leaves their alliance

with love, how is it?

Pages we write and tear

Someone in a swagger coat sits and waits on a hill

It is not spring, may-

be it is never spring

maybe it is the hurt end of summer

the first tender autumn air

fall's first cool rain over the park

and these people walking thru it

The girl thinking:

        life is these pronouns

the man : to ask / to respond / to accept

        bird-life . reindeer-death

        Life is all verbs, vowels and verbs

They both get wet

        If it is love, it is to make

        love, or let be

        'To create the situation / is love

            and to avoid it, this is also

        Love'

as any care or awareness, any

other awareness might   might

        have been

        but is now

hot flesh

socking it into hot flesh

until reindeer-life / bird-death

You are running, see?

you are running down slope across this field

I am running too

to catch you round

This rain is yours

it falls on us

we fall on one another

Belong to the moon

we do not see

It is wet and cool

bruises our skin

might have been

care and avoidance

but we run . run

to prepare

love later

THE MINT QUALITY

One friend—no,

two friends' wives

are near their term and large.

One friend toils

I think that is the word, barren,

still unwed, her

head on what she gave softly

and fiercely wasted   .   Another man

will marry his love in three days' time

and rejoices   .   One

girl is dead   .   No choice

      Christiane dead!   and now again, among

      the white girls, green tender virgins

      who sang under the apple trees, down-

      slope laughing run, hair wet with rain

      naked, between the curve of terrace and the sea

The touch and blackness, down

into the mind and of time, and time-suspended, where

                    hate / love / live

like shadows after that gate closes

                softly

on a daily ration of sun and cloud .

                Sing

                straight as I can.

      In mid-continent, a curve

      on the shoulder of a curve

      sing straight as I can the lines of

      Jaguar the Ship, the broken

beam of a headlight unaccountably turned

           on in

full daylight, staring emptily

           into the ditch.

Not my eyes can see that lovely bitch,

ophelia-hair spread in the shocked water of frogs .

Your spring, Christiane was too short, the

last separation of breath

the dead coal under your heart, our

knowledge of parting, a moan

is the sound of wind in the ship's rigging .

But   HOME, we gladly go home, all my dear friends,

we gladly go into the soil, long feet first, white

face, the nose broken, both eyes blackened, isn't it

      typical? M E R D E !

They picked up my new watch 50   yards away

and time is free for a while—but m e r d e !

all that beautiful eau de vie they shall drink in my honor

and I not get a goddamned drop!

     L e s   s a l a u d s !   All

   right.   I can wait.   But why

did I have to die now?   Given two months more, I would have,

but never mind, I shall be back mes petits, unborn, young,

    de l'âge mûr, entre deux âges,

I had just started life . So you bastards,

I couldn't shut off the ignition and broke my nose .

I'll come back and take my clothes off again,

wait for life to touch me—not too long next time, please .

I am glad to be quiet now for once,

it is cool under the ground, no

lessons to prepare, books to read, nothing to 'arrange'

My mother will not be here before

I'm up again

        singing

filthy songs—my poor mother .

She looks as horrible as I did with red eyes .

        Tout à fait foutue,

        foutue à mort .

        Death is a quiet lover .

        Mother I am glad of death .

Perhaps I'll wait until the end next time

    know what you know

        just to understand .

                I always understand

whenever I feel like it, did you know that?

Freddie made a lovely key for the lock in my headstone,

              some human words:

    "More people should have known her"

—More people will, Freddie,

that key won't turn it shut but open—

key didn't turn off the ignition and broke my nose

    isn't that funny?   Next time maybe

    I'll wait till the middle of life,

        know what you know

            just to understand .

I always understand, didn't you know that?

    In mid-continent

    on the shoulder of a curve of a—

    Roads all over this land

so many more than in France and fewer curves

        You can really go!

        —Sing

straight as I can

under Christiane's cut ration of sun and cloud

which she has left us in, under

the shadow of her clarities

under the shadow of her slender body

seven months gone and dead flesh white with passion

        red with tears

Proud flesh .

the blood drained back

THE CAFÉ FILTRE

Slowly and with persistence

he eats away at the big steak,

gobbles up the asparagus, its

butter & salt & root taste,

drinks at a glass of red wine, and carefully

        taking his time, mops up

    the gravy with bread—

The top of the *café filtre* is

copper, passively shines back, & between

mouthfuls of steak, sips of wine,

     he remembers

   at intervals to

with the flat of his hand

the top removed,

        bang

at the apparatus,

create that suction that

the water will

     fall through

    more quickly

   Across the tiles of the floor, the

   cat comes to the table :   again.

"I've already given you one piece of steak,

what do you want from me now? Love?"

                   He strokes her head, her

rounded black pregnant head, her greedy

    front paws slip from his knee,

        the pearl of great price

        ignored . She's bored, he

bangs the *filtre* again, its top is copper

passively shines back .

                                 Food & wine nearly

finished.

He lifts the whole apparatus off the cup . Merciful

God, will it never be done?   Too cold

                       already

to add cream and sugar, he offers the last

piece of steak with his fingers .

                   She accepts it with calm

                      dignity,

even delicacy . The coffee goes down at a gulp, it

is black

& lukewarm .

IN WINTER

All evidence
of birds is queer, the

square (it is not
square, inter-
section of 9th & 10th Streets, Second Avenue, near

(& within the grounds)
of a church called St. Mark's in-the-Bouwerie
(it is off the Bowery
at least a block off the Bowery)   Bouwerie = -ing farmland
& in this case, the Pieter Stuyvesant farm, well, this square

is
filled
with . young . trees
which in this case on

a minus-20 morning in February, are filled
with sparrows
screaming
as tho this snow were a spring rain somehow

Another day (same month) another
occurrence is clearer :   off the Battery
against an ice-blue sky, some gulls
so soundlessly, the
sound of their wings is all, they
glide above the backs of boats, stern,
up, crying, or surrealisticly quiet .

And .
in the body and wings of each bird . are . go—

SUMMER CLOUDS   /   HIGH AND

SWIFT AGAINST THE HORIZON

or else the snow

THE UNEMPLOYMENT BUREAU

The fly on the floor

of the Unemployment Office

        in Carlisle Street, walks

in quick little spurts as though on wheels, going

      nowhere, circling, tribbling about

      in a circle : when, lash, I

      dash my foot out at him, he

flies a few inches away and lands

          crouched

          sluggish

      then circles back toward my foot

where it stands in line with other unemployed feet

Poor fly,

March is too early in springtime for you to buzz our heads,

black speck on brown tile floor, you

are probably also

trying to get in line.

BRYANT PARK

                    I think it
                    is its
                    location—
                    between 40th & 42nd—
                    gives it its princely
                    quality, by contrast

At the top of the steps in the spring dusk
the sun gone behind
Crompton Velvet & Union Dime, the massive stone
grace of the Public Library at one's back, the
loungers of varying quality on the stone benches
and about one on the steps, across the stairs stretched out
like so many Etruscan statues, old bums, the youngmen, the
college girls with their long legs under short skirts, curled
there on the steps in the fading light   . and below one
the lawn stretching out dark-green velvet all the way to
the fountain near Sixth Avenue, one can almost hear
the sound of falling water between the red and green
light interstices of evening traffic, plash, and at
regular intervals on this edge of lawn, between the
flower beds running an equal length, three signs

        KEEP OFF   KEEP OFF   KEEP OFF

simple enough   . The trees
in lines, doubled at the far sides, have sent
the spring sap up and leaves, the first-broken buds
and moves of green have startled the streetlamps as they
open and see the blood has started up in the dusk, and
there the small leaves are

tender as the legs of girls
opening equally to night and

warm air . The flower beds
splay and tighten the tulips
the hands of men from the Park Department have planted there
in, patterns of triangles, white intersecting the pink and
further down, pink intersecting red isosceles
cut to the side with sun   .   The other bed,
being shade-side, shows only green, the spikes, with
green spikes rising will be flowers tomorrow, next week,
a few white blossoms al-
ready out some halfway down toward the avenue
where buildings rise their own flowers of light, the ugliness
hidden in the new dark   .   I stand

arms parallel to the lines of balustrades, foward, out
stretching as though I were dusk or stone, above the girls, the men
as though my hands were those of the Park Department men, pressing
bulbs into the dark earth months ago, fall of the year,
my stone hands warm with sun, wet and dark with earth, o-
pening, closing, like the flowers all that action will become
tonight for me, now, this evening moment of new leaves and grass.

The lawn stretches out its moment of princely peace .
From the bottom of the steps one
cannot see the bare spots on it, it
stretches out perfect to the eye .
There are those signs . For the moment I am
that tired monarch, that prince after a long day's riding
out for birds or boar or stag . I move my legs
lazily
            twice, and stand

                        at the edge of the grass.

HARK, HARK...

> *ladra, el ladrido,* it
> means barking

—yes, and
this warm spring night, the
dogs do, different dogs
my different voices . and
                           the other sounds : a
man across the vacant lot
laying it down to his wife, the
drunk upstairs thinks he's silently   padding
across the floor in stocking feet, it thumps, it's
                     Friday night

                  "Don' bodderme nomore, yhear?"
             thumps
and the dogs
bark this re-
assuringly peaceful, warm, spring—

The phone rings, it brings a
friend at 6th & Ave. D, beyond
Tompkins Sq. Pk., the other
                           side of town,
& behind the warm voice I hear

a radio on & hear
the dogs bark there

AFFINITIES III.

Walking out of Louis Zukofsky's new place
Columbia Heights
at 1:35 in the morning
there's the smell of sea
the sound of boats / that turn of the bay
                    into river and up
crossing, the engines over the night, the
night over the bridge, the bridge
                    over the river and

up
2 blocks
the smell of all that goes
into memory of itself until, by Hicks St. the only
real thing is the odor of already-walked dogs and one's own
sweat in the summer night.

            How keep this thief from home
            and the guard down
            for a moment?

                    to turn back, to
                    make harbor at that,
                    that moment of crossing.

AN ATMOSPHERE,

                              or how

put it to you, render.

Tender is the.

Past has some dignity after all,

that is its re-al—its

                              virtue, that you

hold it close, hold it

CLOSE, whatever I give you

you gave it first . It's

not hard to celebrate the sky

But I heard the bus come thru the block, the

bus after your bus, come

thru.

Two cats yowled, the starfish

held out its five arms

PHONE CALL TO RUTHERFORD

"It would be—
                a mercy if
you did not come see me . . .

"I have dif-fi / culty
                speak-ing, I
cannot count on it, I
am afraid it would be too em-
                ba
                rass-ing
for me   ."

                —Bill, can you still
                answer letters?

"No . my hands
are tongue-tied . You have . . . made

a record in my heart.
                Goodbye."

                                                Oct 1962

THE STONE

The stone found me in bright sunlight
around 9th and Stuyvesant Streets and
found, if not a friend, at
least a travelling companion.
Kicking we crossed
Third Avenue, then Cooper Square, a-

voiding the traffic in our oblique and
random way, a cab almost got him, and I had
to wait a few seconds, crowding
in from the triangular portion edged about
with signs, safety island, crossed
Lafayette, him catching between the cobbles, then
with a judicious blow
from the toes of my foot (right) well, a
soccer kick aiming for height we cleared
the curb and turned left down Lafayette,
that long block,
with a wide sidewalk and plenty of room to maneuver
in over metal cellar doorways or swinging
out toward the curb edge. The low worn
curb at 4th was a cinch to make, and
at Great Jones Street the driveway into a
gas station promised no impediment. But
then he rolled suddenly to the right
as though following an old gentleman in a long
coat, and at the same time I was addressed
by a painter I know and his girl on their way
to Washington Square, and as I looked up to
answer,
I heard the small sound. He had fallen
in his run, into water gathered in a sunken
plate which they lift to tighten or loosen
something to do with the city water supply I think,
and sank out of sight.
I spoke to Simeon and D.
about a loft it turned out he hadn't gotten, but
felt so desolate at having lost him they didn't
stay long, I looked at the puddle, explained
we'd come all the way from beyond Cooper Square,

they hurried away.

I suppose I could have used my hands, picked him
out and continued, he'd have been dry by the time
we got home, but just as I decided to abandon him
the sun disappeared.

I continued on down Bleecker finally,
a warm front moving in from the west, the
cirrus clotting into alto-cumulus, sun seeping through
as the front thickened, but not shining, the air turned
cool, and there were pigeons
circling
over the buildings at
West Broadway, and over them a gull, a
young man with a beard and torn army jacket walked
a big mutt on a short leash teaching him to heel.
The mutt was fine, trotting alongside, nuzzling
lightly at his master's chino pants, the young
man smiled, the dog smiled too, and on they went.
They had each other.

I had left him there in the puddle, our game
over, no fair using hands I had told myself.

Not that he could have smiled.

The sun gone in.

He had been shaped like a drunken pyramid, ir-
regularly triangular.

I liked him.

IT MIGHT AS WELL BE SPRING

6:15
is already dark on
a winter night
    in December, remember? You
    keep coming back like a song
    in January, I sed you

j a n - u - w a r y . sunset is five-forty-seven .

    "Ven I kom to dis country
    skirts vair *dis* high
           (the hand)
    und vit a slit, yet, in da zide,
    up to *here!*"

    I can't look.
Out the steamed-up window instead, a pickup truck is
cream-colored and dark avocado-green in the street
streaked every few minutes or so with pale yellow headlights
uptown on the avenue . The pickup
truck apparently delivers instead . Out of the
deli next door, figure of a man, stalks the truck, opens
the door of the truck .

    In the window, it
being night, the inside of the bakery-restaurant is
    reflected back . The waitress
is cleaning up the dishes three tables back . Watch,
    the crotch,
near where her hand lay to indicate the height (D E P T H?)
    of the slit in the dress, the
uniform is white, tight, it's night, the man
    outside opens the truck door
and climbs into the waitress's skirt
    very naturally, and
          just below the waist .

Neither one knows,
but it might as well be spring .

RITUAL IX. : GATHERING WINTER FUEL

The jews burn wood on First Ave., New York City, in a

barrel, to keep

w a r m

Clayton's

workmen across the cut

their house in Kyoto, likewise

warming their hands, the same cans or barrels, in the dark

flames leaping, men standing around, and

I have seen it on the West Side, New York, Gansevoort Street

growing up among the meat packers there, would go

out

at night

hunting wooden crates

break up for the fireplace

to keep w a r m , my

mother's hands those days,

warming her arthritic smile . hands

& I myself in that

furnished room on 15th Street that had a fireplace, I

knew where to go to score for crates

/ Good

king Wenceslas went out

gath-er-ing

on St. Stephen's day

winter fee-yew-well, or

the vacant lot at Houston

between Mott & Third

the same barrels

& cans & older men in long

overcoats from the mission,

& here the scene unabated / 20-odd years later

the fruit & vegetable market, First Avenue & Ninth, using

wood from crates

New Jersey, Delaware, Cali-

for-ni-yay,

Florida, New Mexico, Georgia, Louisiana, Texas, all

for the same fire, how

reunite the South and North, the West and East—

w a r m ,

in sunlight you never see it, just

walking by &

feel the warmth . there .

Fire in a barrel, burning

the hands, the hands, the italian

bakery next door is still discreet,

but the kosher butchershop next to

that comes out for a word or two, the

gesture,

palms stiff out at arms' length, passing

the time of day, their magic   h a n d s

liverspotted and reddened maybe, no paesas or beard, still

here at First Avenue and Ninth Street, it's

the jews uniting the world, the country, the city,

mankind down geological time perhaps,

to keep their hands warm .

THIS IS NOT THE SAME AS SHARING ANYONE ELSE'S DESPAIR

BRIGHT   SUNLIGHT
on the avenue
Green & cream

the buses,
red & cream, the buses .
black . beige . red & cream
black . beige . red & cream

the cars

uptown .

Black dog in a red harness

looks in at the door .
Old man
out of harness, looks

in, at the door .

"I haven't seen one of 'em yet .

I haven't seen one like'm yet,"
says Aunt Ella looking out the door

/

"My old man."

You can tell by the tone she means her
                              husband.
              "Since he died,"
                              she continues,
        "I   H A V E N ' T   M E T   A N Y O N E   E L S E / "

Aunt Ella's cross is people, don't
know the names of things .

          "Is that carroway seed?"   asks a lady
          in a fur coat better than most. "No,
                          them's poppyseeds," says Aunt
Ella, & to the first conversation, confirming,   "that's
why I never married again . Fifteen,
twenny dollas a night he usta spend."

                          Very loud.

Old woman with kerchief round her head &
had come in holding one hand over the heart,
                          the man's tweed jacket, the
                          heart she is wearing, sends
                          the barley soup back

"It is
too salty,"   she says.
The cook sends back a cream of potato
soup.
Over which she is silent, but makes eating noises .
Her face is half-eaten away .
Aunt Ella still on the register :
the guy two tables away hits the Saturday-waitress for

ten . He's her boyfriend

and's eating free . He

wears a cream nylon tie

with blue & red stripes & a midnite-blue jacket .

The tie is terrible

She loves him . Aunt

Ella to her interlocutor in

an old army overcoat & grey hair,

from no context

shouts reflectively,

"S o m e d a y ! "

Bright sunlight on the avenue

Green & cream, the buses,

red & cream, the buses .

black . beige . red & cream

black . beige . red & cream

the cars

uptown .

PRE-LENTEN GESTURES

Thank God one tone or

one set of decibels is

not all there is.   The

Dies Irae, the radio behind me, is,

due to the mad programmer we never know, followed

by a selection of military band music.

How kind.   I

can't help thinking of

Ed Dorn, his line: *Why*

can't it be like this all the time?

"as my friend said"

the band, the binding, the

bound from one state to the next, and sometimes

one is not even asked.

What may be revealed, given.

What?

that it be revealed.

A girl comes in with her little fur hat

and wants to buy   T H A T

cake that looks like a group of buns in the window.

Impulse buying.   That's what it is, a group of buns.

Her young husband stands outside in

his little fur hat, smiling, superciliously.

"Foolish little girl,"

said Rudolph Valentino, smiling

to himself on the set as he read and pocketed

the bill from his tailor.

"What is it called?"

"Sugar buns," says Aunt Ella

looking at the buns themselves

as tho she were identifying some obscure layer

of geological time for a

micro-paleontologist who might know better, that her

expression not insult the girl.

"35¢" says Aunt Ella.

The girl drops a dime of the change, leaving.

Her little

husband in the door smiles as she bends

to pick it up.

Boy in a nicely shaped black coat and a package of

laundry, crook of his arm, who has been

not-quite-studying the menu on the window between them

glances to his left and disappears down the avenue

as the girl emerges,

readjusts his bundle.

Aunt Ella runs the squeegee over the length of the door,

the glass steamed so .   it is revealed

that the red blotch

on the opposite curb is a Jaguar (cap J)

and the blue one behind it's a Ford.

Robin's-egg Ford

O n w a r d   a n d   u p w a r d ,

we used to say in the army, before

trying to pick up a cluster of teenagers, the

streets of San Antone that hot,

we were that hot   .   A small boy has started a fire

in the vacant lot beyond the Jaguar and Ford.   Sousa

still calling the sounds from the radio at my back.

I   AM   BACK   to an earlier question:

someone had found it strange

I should think of the concomitant physical cul-

      mination of love,

fucking, in short, as a release, some

    times a relief from

  the pain of loving itself.

Surcease of pain. The idea

     is medieval at least:

"o lady, give me some relief,

cure me of that sweet sickness

I am subject to"

     object, of course,

      bed   .   what

happens to impulses from fingers that touch that

smooth skin, that they skim the breast, down the

line of ribs, beneath the indentation of waist, the

flare of hip, smoothness of thigh rounding inward

past forests of night to churn among mucous membranes,

heat rising.

The beaky crane, the

"one-eyed great goose"

the tower risen out of the olive grove.

Surcease of pain.

Love, the disease that implies

its own cure, part and end of it.

And that end begins again.

"You, who alone can cure me by your touch, Lady,"

a cry they sometimes insisted was, had been

addressed to the Virgin, implied in its end

surcease of pain, no virgin, but another hand,

and that miraculous touch his lady's fingers curled

against his own, against the small of his back, flat out.

A mystery? No . What

else could happen?   The

world is what it is, men and women what they are.

Every organic thing, o philosophers, man,

plant or animal, containing as seed the flower,

its own destruction, its own rebirth . Yeats was right?

"All true love must die

Alter at the best

Into some lesser thing.

Prove that I lie."

Hardly,

with O'Leary in the grave, seed of that growth,

cure of that ill, and

once begun, the act fore-

tells its own, what-

ever-breaking-now, its own

      end . revealed.

      Squeegee drawn once more

    down the door's glass,

the Jaguar gone, the Ford remains itself at last,

revealed smaller now by itself, as the houses, parks,

the football fields of our youth, than

        it / they / then /

        seemed .

    It always is,

    always was

    this way, Ed,

    all the time.

It is not that it does not happen.

It does,

      and there is no help for it.

      And

there is no end to it,

until there is .

OBIT PAGE

O god.

First the greatest right-handed batter in history

Rogers Hornsby

              (hit   .424 in   1924)

        with a lifetime average of   .358

and now   William Carlos Williams

                                       Jan 5
                                       Mar 4
                                       1963

From THE SELECTION OF HEAVEN

1.   GOD,   that it did happen,
       that loose now, that
       early configuration
              of birds, the texture set in
              words,   1945,
       a Staten Island beach in early October

here in more than flesh and brick,
9th Street, March 1963.

    The clouds were love.
    The words we have near 18 years, you
    prophesy, it could have been that,
    the bullshit
    words, if that is what we are then,
    that they can
          do, come to
    Life .
        You
    put that much life in it, baby,
    you know you can't win   (touch
          bottom to darkness where)

This grey . soft . overcast . not-quite-rainy day,
that I can
swim my mind in it, swim it in overcast, the sun
tries, and there they are, the birds, my gulls
circle over a street to the North.

In the street below a child's voice yells
"Kick'm in the nuts . . . . . kick'm in the nuts!"
        broadcast :
        Allen K. says
    you have to let a man have all
             /
                 his balls.
    I am afraid he speaks from experience.
And here the small birds sing
speak from experience, outside
      my window, come   .

And my big birds, my gulls, come
here   .   I see them here, I
can walk thru it,
              swim it.

2.   ROYAL EBONY
     is the name of a carbon paper . Is
     also title of a poem by Nicolás Guillén.

     The smoke rises in a thread, a
     curled stream from between
     his thumb and forefinger
     as he snuffs it out.
                    We live.
                    Pity?   It
                    is the waste of their lives.

     No.   Pity is hate.
             Pity is hate.
                    Pity is hate.
     Pity
     is
     hate.
             O,   were it so,
     or as they say,
     were it not so.

3.   HOW do we keep any of it

                    ever?   Do you

know what I'm talking about?
You borrow my books
you borrow my bicycle
7:30 A.M.   Sunday morning
to ride to Staten Island with
a girlfriend.   Yes you know.

Love
is different each time we taste it .

4.   MESTIZA: brown, olive and black.
Scudding clouds the sun rides against.
The wind wins   /   brown, olive, and black
wind of bicycle-March against her jacket
shape of her top
revealed
                    /
                 the legs push   .   It is not
July, heatwaves rising from a blacktop road,
it is March   .   the sun wins sometimes,
a few minutes .   Staten
Island, yes, my gulls are there, the wind, their
generations later of grandchildren
                         nesting soon

mestiza : brown, olive and black.
The gulls are white and black
                    simply   /   sun
catches the underwing
clouds keep moving
                    .   If you
            watch clouds, riding
a bicycle is dizzying

The smoke rises in a thread
from between his thumb
and middlefinger.

5.   March 3, 1 A.M. / Kyoto.

After the conversation in two voices
after the poems
a list of objects around you
no
collage but a set of emblems
blazing low as the tea stays hot
growling from the fire
the walls   .   wood and rock
surround you
your sleeping woman, that
softness   .   *The Harbor Dawn*
not preceded by Te Deum . . . . Hand of Fire
not followed by macadam gun-grey as
your own dawn comes
                              /
                        Buzz
of the plane, hark
Hart, high, small, and distinct
The heart of clay
is shared, baked and
brittle tho it may not break.

That day does break   .   My
gulls were never further away
than this   .   The sun
coming and
coming

6. ÁSHARA :

es la siguiente : a
myth-real term in Japanese:
in Arabic it is the number   10
Color is black   .   "the warring,
hostile, contentious aspect of the mind"
Black is the crow
from the still-white ground to the
black branch, is
the black of cypress spires in the graveyard of Béziers,
is the blackness of night out across the cut
those two spotlights out, the
hours before the dawn
light reading to the cats outside
the cats prowling, the
tape spinning
slowly, at   3¾ ips
the cat here in my window
black as hell is, black,
as crow, as cypresss, down
into the mind and time suspended is
how this color is, is no color, is
black crow,
'black cat, black
cypresses in dawn sky, is
black as black is, is the
sound of sea, the wings flapping.
Gulls are white   . sins . The mind
is
dark .
"Full fathom five thy father lies"
it is
the number   10
Color is black.

7. THE MERE
    concordance of these sufferings :
                        Hannah died.
    Tomorrow the funeral in New Bedford, Mass.,
    the interment, the last dancing of the coffin,
    shadow of birdflight flash across the box, the
    ground is cold, should we see it, in Fairhaven—
    cross the river, turn
    down toward the bay   .   Hannah
    Gibbs Whiting Mackey Blackburn died,
    87, after a full life .   I,
    grandson, 37,   (you
    gauge there those fifty years, I know
                    the small dif-
    ferences, way they ought, or
    not too far wrong—)   away,
                        Ruth,
    Sarruth.
    You are that young,
    too young   .   We never have
    until tonite, given
    that grey gentleness
    to one another   .   wet, yes,
    and why not?
    Tell me what else this shoulder might serve for
    please, I want to live beyond that
    please, the drive back   300   miles
    please, the ground is cold, there is
    please, no other life, please,
    please there IS that
    difference, say it
    might have been a man but
    now, no care, who

could care?   it was that dif-

  (small dif-)

   erence be-

tween the man who filled was

more a child   .   You can

turn your back

or I can turn my back—

     it is a child

unborn, it is our being

all our being

man and wife, or else the rest

of life is Jack the

life is back, is fact, is black, is

rope enuf, is no rope, is the ripper

    is the ripper

    is the ripper

is the child, un-

born perhaps,

    and sucking.

    . . .

16.   w o r d s : should have been spoken at graveside

There are no true voices anymore, John

Henry, you knucklehead, you hard-

headed, stiff-backed, tough-minded old man, your

    mouth is clenched tight for good

    it is a solid line

from under your sharpened nose around your pointed chin, above

          that

the strong, kind, (remembered), and finally closed eyes,

the dead tissues under the skull that were your brain

softened finally with your   88   years

into a forgetfulness your children could
relate to, could pity, could and did
expiate themselves upon, so
                    accept their own lives

for what they had become or grown to,
John, you knucklehead, you bonehead, in
the old photographs you are more often
                    scowling, when the others
are smiling bravely into the bright sun.

                    You quarreled
with everyone you loved and were proud
when your children fought you back with brain and spirit
and were hurt, of course you were hurt
                    by it, and loved them   .   You
had made them irrevocably yours you would have said God's

and that's not true, and your mouth is closed for good
upon the air of this world, your hands   not
                    folded in eternity as that
                    cliché-ridden, pompous, minister
friend of yours who did you final service might
have said had he the gift of words, but
clenched, holding your heaven to you;
swollen farmer's hands that had been kinder than your mind was
clenched in eternity the rock of your mind
that could not crack and open but
still clenched dissolved under the rain of years

the head still,
straight white hair still handsome   .   4
generations gathered round a coffin yesterday to pay

what truly was respect and sometimes love,   the
different qualities of flesh

                        from ruined to what

                  renews itself each day, and grows, John,

stood there and did you honor   .   Rocks

wear away under the rain   .   Flesh is tough
    the spirit
resilient   .   tougher than flesh   .   They
said you looked natural
and in their mouths it
was comforting cliché   .   The words
were truer than they knew, you still looked
              stiff-backed, hard-headed,
              but the spirit gone, that blur,
a peace   .

EARTH TO EARTH

GOD,
be here at this graveside .
Not in the cut flowers the undertakers' men heaped up
but in the new forsythia, red maple
              buds, magnolia, be
              in the spring earth
will heap this grave, grow new grass over it,
golden green of willow starting fresh . be
              in the spring earth with John,
your faithful servant,
where he will lie
next to Hannah as he did in life, her
              eternal lover   .   Lock them
              forever into this hillside

facing the Acushnet gulls settle on,

    wheel over crying, hear them in the

distance .

    Smoke rises

from between my forefinger

and middlefinger   .   Wind on this

cold spring hillside sweeps it off

barely visible in the sunlight

the ashes

fall upon new grass .

A S H E S   T O   A S H E S

    John,

forgive the carpet of phoney grass

          too dark for the season

the undertakers spread beneath your

coffin for this moment . We have

seen you to this hillside, let it be

enough   .   Forgive

the Reverend Doctor his recitation

of   2   Edgar Guest poems yesterday,   I

figured I could stand it if you could . The rain

    of dirt and pebbles will be real enough .

              fresh clods set in

          after you have settled   .   Rain

             fructifies,

            but will wear away .

           ROCK

The committing ceremony had the
dignity of its own
                    words, yesterday,
despite the use of flowers with their snapped-off heads
instead of fistfuls of earth   .   EARTH   .
When the diggers end the job, let
the first   3   shovelsful of spring earth
be my shovelsful, let it be enough   .

DUST TO DUST

                    consigning   .   I

have not willed the occasion for these words
which cry themselves like hunting gulls
my mouth flapping open   .   GOD,
welcome your servant John Henry
into whatever Paradise he thought existed,
offer him
the best accomodation that you have for such a
                    lover of the mind   .   God
                    knows he has earned it,
               twice over   .
Let there be soft
               wind
where he is, let him hear gulls cry
above the
bridge,
               and be home.

1963–67

TWO SONGS FOR THE OPP

1. Stay drunk!

  that's my motto .

  Then you'll never have to know

  if the girl love you or no

      (hee hee hee

       nor will she

2. Play gui-

  tar, go to the bar

  hope there's one hand will caress

  and undress

  But pints to go

  before you sleep

      (har, har,

       nobody care

GRAFFITI

The New York Public Library at one's back...

and a statue of William Cullen Bryant
(1794-1878)

around & back of which are
newspapers, bottles : Gallo,
Arriba, Thunderbird, Banner
Port, Twister, & Gypsy Rose
and inscribed on the stone:

"Yet let
no empty dust
of passion find an utterance in thy lay,
a blast that whirls the dust
along the howling street and dies away;
but feelings of calm power and mighty sweep
like currents journeying through the windless deep."

It also says
in less en-
during form:

CRICKET & VINCENT   FRANK LOVES MARGE

Stacey and Troy   ERIC & TORCH

BEV AND TOM   daphne & rickie

then: Daphne & Boys!

also: DIANE LOVES BOYS

poor Daphne, but
Lourdes & Joey FOREVER

The earliest dates
are 1961 .

THE WATCHERS

It's going to rain
Across the avenue a crane
whose name is
      CIVETTA LINK-BELT
dips, rises and turns in a
    graceless geometry

    But grace is slowness   /   as
ecstasy is some kind of speed or madness   /
The crane moves slowly, that
much it is graceful   /   The men
    watch and the leaves

Cranes make letters in the sky
    as the wedge flies
        The scholar's function is

            Mercury, thief and poet,
            invented the first   7   letters,
            5   of them vowels, watching
            cranes   .   after got

The men watch and the rain does not come
        HC – 108B CIVETTA LINK-BELT
In the pit below a yellow cat,
      CAT – 933
                pushes the debris
and earth to load CIVETTA HC – 108B
    Cat's name is PASCO and
    there is an ORegon phone number,
moves its load toward   3   piles
Let him leave the building to us

    Palamedes, son of Nauplius,
    invented   11   more
                (consonant)
    Also invented the lighthouse, and
    measures, the scales, the disc, and
    "the art of posting sentinels"
    Ruled over the Mysians,

Cretan stock, al-
though his father was Greek
Took part in the Trojan trouble on the
Greek side . The scholar's function is fact   . Let him
quarry cleanly .   All
T H O S E   I N V E N T I O N S   C R E T A N
so that a Greek   /   alpha-beta-tau
based on a Cretan, not a Phoenician
model
Three different piles :

earth   /   debris   /   & schist, the stud/stuff of the island
is moved by this
PASCO
CAT – 933
ORegon 6–
it does not rain   .   smoke, the
alpha-beta-tau

raised from   5   vowels, 13 consonants to
5   vowels, 15 consonants
(Epicharmus)   not
the Sicilian writer of comedies, 6 A.D., but
his ancestor   /
the Aesculapius family at Cos, a couple are
mentioned in the Iliad as physicians to
the Greeks before the equipotent walls
of Troy

No, it does not rain, smoke
rises from the engines, the
leaves .   The men watch
before the walls of Troy

Apollo in cithaera ceteras literas adjecit

7   strings on that zither
& for each string a letter
Thence to Simonides,
native of Ceos in the service of Dionysus
which god also at home in Delphos
both gods of the solar year as were   /   Aesculapius
& Hercules
Let's
get all of this into one pot, 6-700 years B.C.

Simonides, well-known poet, intro-
ducted into Athens   4   more letters .   the
    unnecessary double-consonants *PSI*
                      (earlier written Pi-Sigma)

    and *XI*   (earlier written Kappa-Sigma)
plus (plus) two vowels : *OMEGA*, a distinction from
    t h e   o m i c r o n   H e r m e s   c o n n e d
    f r o m   t h e   3   C r o n e s ,   a n d
EPSILON, as distinct from their eta
& that's the long & the short of it .

Cranes fly in V-formation & the
Tyrrhenians, or Etruscans, were
also of Cretan stock, held
the crane in reverence   /   The men watch
                      LINK-BELT move up its load, the
                      pile to the left near 24th St., the
                      permanent erection moves
                      slow-ly, almost sensually, al-most
                                gracefully
The scholar's function   /   fact .   Let him quarry
cleanly   /   leave the building to us   /   Poems
nicked with a knife onto the bark of a stick (Hesiod)
    or upon tablets of clay
              Perseus cuts off the Gorgon-head
                (Medusa)
              and carries it off in a bag . But
the head's a ritual mask and a protection, we
frighten children with it
and trespassers
when we perform the rites . It is
                          no murder,
                          she has given him power of sight

p o e t r y ,
            the gorgons no pursuers
            are escort, and the mask
                  (his protection)
Hermes / Car / Mercury / Perseus / Palamedes / Thoth / or
    whatever his original name was,
winged sandals and helmet, you bet!
the swiftness of poetic thought   /   And the bag

T H E   A L P H A B E T ' S   I N   T H E   B A G !

Almost sensually, almost
gracefully   .   The men watch
and know not what they watch
The cat pushes . the crane   .   the bud
lifts upward   .   above the

                    Pillars of Hercules, desti-
nation, where he is going, bringing the secret in the bag
              The tree at Gades (Cádiz)
        principal city of Tartessus, the
Aegean colony on the Guadalquivir
F r o m   t h e r e   t h e   M i l e s i a n s   w i l l   t a k e   i t   t o   I r e l a n d
T h e   o l d e r   c i t y   i s   o n   t h e   w e s t e r n   s h o r e   w i t h   i t s
        Temple of Cronus   .   island,
        the island of the goddess,
        Red Island   /   & Cronus
god of the middle finger, the fool's finger   /   It is
        his father he kills not his mother, his mother
        gives him
              the secret
                    Scholar's function is
                              The men watch

Hercules' shrine set up by colonists, 1100 B.C.
400   years before the Phoenicians
coming from Tyre in painted ships
        and their oracle
                    HERCULES = PALAMEDES (?)

7   &   2
9   steps to the goddess
& everyone lives to 110 years
5   years to a lustrum
                    (Etruscan)
22   lustra   =   110
                    (alpha-beta-tau
& the circumference of the circle when
        the diameter is   7   is
22
proportion known as π
22 (plus) over   7
a neat recurrent sequence
which does not work out because it never
ends   /
7   lustra is   35   years   .   Maturity,
or the age at which a man may be elected

President of the United States / a convention
or a Roman might be elected Consul   /   a convention
$$\frac{22}{7}$$
These numbers no longer a secret   /   But in Crete
                                          or Spain . . .
Spanish, the mother's family name
still is set down last, and
still in Crete descent is matrilineal
The Greeks have accomplished nothing
          but death   beauty
               (Troy)
T h e   m e n   w a t c h   t h e   c a t   p u s h
k e e p i n g   t h e   p i l e s   d i s c r e t e
e a r t h   /   d e b r i s   /   &   s c h i s t
t h e   s t u f f   o f   t h e   i s l a n d ,   t h e   c r a n e ,   t h e   b u d
l i f t s   u p w a r d   .   a b o v e   t h e

                              And at Cádiz, Caius Julius Hyginus,
                              a Spaniard and Ovid's friend,
                              curator of the Palatine Library,
                              exiled from the court of Augustus

sitting under a tree in Cádiz
over the problem, over a millenium later,
traces Greek letters in the spelt of wine at his table
watches the cranes fly over toward Africa
wedge in the sunset   /   set down the score :

                    Mercury (or the Fates)   7
                    Palamedes   11
                    Epicharmus   2
                    Simonides   4
Say that he used Etruscan sources,
     does that explain it?
Let them quarry cleanly
     Let them leave
Cranes winging over toward Africa
     a wedge .
Hyginus traces   π   on the wooden table in wine spelt

     The cat pushes, the crane, the bud
     lifts upward   /   above the
     rain comes finally
The watchers leave the construction site,

the men leave their machines
    At 323 Third Avenue,
    an old drunk (Hyginus)
sits in a doorway and downs a whole
pint of Sacramento Tomato Juice

            The watchers are the gods

            The leaves burgeon

SUNDOWN . THE LAST OF THE WINE

Red wine, half-a-bottle I had
found in the surf at Bridgehampton
in the afternoon
        COOL FROM THE SEA

Al tasted it with me .

Evening   .   sundown   .
            mockup of the day :

having slammed my left thumb in the car door

I cut myself on the can opener

        opening hot beer .

God knows it might have happened to anyone.

Only
the beachday over, I
slipped on the steps of the ho-tel
      and had to
use my sprained right arm to catch
           with to
save the delicate joining membranes of
the carapace of deathshead monster horseshoe crab

I had found on the beach,

had saved from the day, the tide.

HERE THEY GO

The little lights in the alley
great arclights on the bridges
        and the edges of parks.
                                The young
are beautiful, walking past in the dark, in the
night, couples, two pairs, three,
children alone   .   Children   .

                They've a different world than we had, more
                        brilliant, darker .
                Hip or unhip, there's the same thing
                that edge of warm light ahead of them .
                Darkness they know   .   yes, they
                know the isolations   .   come   .

Some,
fearing the example of their parents, are
afraid to love   .   others fearing
the example of their parents,

are helpless before the emotion, not
believing it possible.

                "I'm   16   years old," says one girl, "and
                never been kissed.
                "But I make it once in a while."

The generation,
or two if you like, ahead of them
uses deodorants.
                They, tho,
                like the smell of hot flesh
                suffering relief of its passion .

Sloppy and full of bravado they will live beyond us .
Their cocks dripping helplessly
their cunts full of sperm .

                Two classes of Hunter High School girls
                came to a recommended M.D.
                        to be fitted for diaphragms, ac-
                                                (knowledged

companied by their mothers .
The M.D. felt better about her son
who dated sometimes
girls from Hunter HS.

                                        Little lamps in the alley
                                        streetlights in Brooklyn
                                        like any midwestern town:
protect the young from their elders

                                        while,
            a lo mejor, they fuck
close, or at worst go down on each other .
business of hands for the tender
            touch at least
                        they
                                    the night

Great arclights at the edges of parks
along bridges, Manhattan to Brooklyn
                    or the other way .
                                        (Where are you?
The sodium flares
make public
the new world rising
from the dark waters

from dark grass .

BARREL ROLL

                        PECK SLIP   .   smell of wholesale coffee
                                    floating in from Beekman, fish, a
wail of improbable proportions, tug
                        on the East River .
                Bar is called THE PARIS   .   Bell & Co.,
                        RING FISH, the
ring on my finger, my
toes parched on the stones.

Bells and whistles from the river.
The gulls circle and ride the wind above the bridge.
One

rides it as slowly as possible,

the line of his wings, leading-edge up

folding against it

not soaring, no

ecstasy, that hold, so

slow he moves in the glide, tension of wing strut,
those bones

holding suddenly, suddenly

doing a   b a r r e l   r o l l   not losing altitude .

the control .

ON THE ROCKS

Small,
Polish they told him, bar, East 7th Street
Saturday nights
is the only one still open after 2 A.M.
hence

crowded   .   to so prowl   .

Even crowded is cool and quiet:
the bowling machine in one corner keeps the score
with little clicks, sighs, and bells, the

jukebox down the wall turned down from concert size
no blare   .   the bar

packed, tables in the back near-empty .

JUKEBOX: Slav, Slovene, Russian, Polish, Hun-
garian, all that lonely, impassioned
schwarze zigeuner, the violin catguts
to tear the heart if it be torn already.

Whose is not?

Ø

Midsummer madness by the sea at night, *las*
olas doblandose siempre
                    knees dug into the cool sand
                    Couples spread out between the
rocks hiding from the beams of
policecars patrolling boardwalk

            He arranges the blanket properly
                    properly
            waves slosh among the rocks

One feels an intruder and walks
            away
            slowly
            back
toward the lights, the light surf repe-
titious,   dull in the ear .

                The lovers will swim forever.
                The whole night.

        Ø

            Coming out of the bar, slosh, the waves, lovers
            sleep lightly, their hot life away for a while, their
            arms, coming out of the bar violins, gulls sleep
                    on the waves
                    cry at his back
            until the door closes   .   streets wet
                                    the summer rain

Reflections more shimmering and real than
the lights, dull surf, than any wall
where the mind goes blank .

THE ART

to write poems, say,

is not a personal achievement

that bewilderment

On the way to work

two white butterflies

& clover along the walks

to ask .

to want that much of it .

AT THE WELL

Here we are, see?
in this village, maybe a camp
middle of desert, the
Maghreb, desert below Marrakesh
standing in the street
simply.

        Outskirts of the camp
        at the edge of town, these riders
        on camels or horses,
        but riders, tribesmen, sitting
        there   on their horses.

                They are mute.   They are
                hirsute, they are not
                able to speak. If they
                could the sound would be gutteral.
                They cannot speak. They want
                something.

I nor
you know what they want   .   They want
nothing.   They are beyond want.   They need
nothing.   They used to be slaves.   They
want something of us   /   of me   /   what
shall I say to them.

They have had their tongues cut out.
I have nothing to give them   ¿There is no
grace at the edge of my heart I would grant,
render them?   They want something, they
sit there on their horses.   Are there
children in the village I can give them.

> My child's heart? Is it goods they want
> as tribute. They have had their tongues
> cut out. Can I offer them some sound
> my mouth makes in the night?   Can I
> say they are brave, fierce, im-
> placable? that I would like to
> join them?

Let us go together

across the desert toward the
cities, let us
terrify the towns, the villages,
disappear among bazaars, sell our
camels, pierce our ears, for-
get that we are mute and drive
the princes out, take all the
slave-girls for ourselves?
What can I offer them.

> They have appeared here on the edge of my soul.
> I ask them what they want, they say
> —You are our leader.   Tell us what
> your pleasure is, we
> want you.   They
> say nothing.   They

are mute.   they are hirsute.   They
are the fathers I never had.   They are
tribesmen standing on the edge of town near
water, near the soul I must look into each
morning   .   myself.

> Who are these wild men?
> I scream:
> —I want my gods!

                    I want my goods!   I want
         my reflection in the sun's pool at morning,
              shade in the afternoon under the
                  date palms, I want and want!

What can I give them.
What tribe of nomads and wanderers am I continuation of, what
can I give my fathers?
What can I offer myself?

                    I want to see my own skin
                    at the life's edge, at the
                    life-giving water.   I want
                    to rise from the pool,
                    mount my camel and
         be among the living, the other side of this village.

Come gentlemen,
wheel your mounts about.
There is nothing here .

24 . II . 64
NOTE TO KYOTO

Clay, it is almost spring .   the air

is polar, tho, and the nights clear.

Even in the warrens of the city I look for you

for her   for you   I look

at stars over the parks,

brick

steel

glass

bodies

god, and

there   a r e   stars

    &   12 hours later there you are

under the great Asian night,

hands in your pockets, walking

the roads to come to your hot tea, the fire in your house .

It's spring again old man, it's coming steep against my

nerves, the old sap roiling up

makes me sick again to go

            out   /   I want

                to go   .   Paris!

        Barcelona in a single leap!

expanding like a star out over the Atlantic night

L'ORCUS

Long sideburns & teeth showing,

the teeth showing, seedy boy,

      overcoat slack, he's back,

      that figure of joy

to offer the subway system & everyone on it

           this 1 A.M., of

           April 9, 1964

           seeds,

or what it / I / they / we /

needs .

NIGHT CAPPY

O, Danny Lynch be sittin below there in McSorley's

having an India Pale & a porter & a bit o' conver-

sation & I

not joinin him, what whith his black eye an' all .

        Instead,

        I come direct up to bed,

        wheer the wife do be readin the newspaper

        & don't even move over for me .

I understand what the solution is, but

what be the question ?

He t'ought it were a weddin but

it was a funeral   .   So ?

        what is the question . or,

        who is a friend of the groom ?

LISTENING TO SONNY ROLLINS AT THE FIVE-SPOT

THERE WILL be many other nights like
be standing here with someone, some
one
someone
some-one
some
some
some
some
some
some
one
there will be other songs
a-nother fall, another—spring, but
there will never be a-noth, noth
anoth
noth
anoth-er
noth-er
noth-er
        Other lips that I may kiss,
but they won't thrill me like
      thrill me like
           like yours
used to
     dream a million dreams
but how can they come
when there
       never be
a-noth—

CALL IT THE NET

Imagine a young woman

lying on her back at the intersection

Third Ave. and 8th St., at Astor Place, no,

      not fallen, but on her back,

reclining there in the snow, looking

alive, up at the passing crowd, they

part afraid to look but those that do,

      the men,

she raises an amorous clouding of their eyes.

      It is a threshold I cross, no

      longer an intersection, the bird

hidden in the shirt upon the chest

torn   .   the eye

swells in the head

bird flutters and falls into the sea of eyes

      She was so beautiful

Bird and sun are holy take the head

tear it open and set it like a

melon upon the threshold   .

          I cross   .   Everything

that lives, Blake says, is holy   .   yes

Bird, sun, eyes, the street, the inter-

section, the fish (hip) swims from between my legs,

LEAPS, yes, that was a year ago.

        But that silken trap.

Love drinks itself and is drunk.

The girl gets up off her back

and walks off quick, a clust-er

of sparrows bursts from the intersection into

            grey sky   .

The eyes around the bed I sleep in

           watch   .   That silken trap

Fucking drunk   .   Over the cold shadow of the street

        running.

        After her.

Call it the net of lust   .

THE NET OF MOON

           Impact of these splendid

things

upon the appropriate sense

How

refuse to meddle with them, how seem

to hide our passion in the dance of

moon upon the small waves, how come to it hugely

erected and keep, we tell ourselves, a just balance be-

tween the emotion and motion of wave on the bay, the

leap of the dolphin in our dreams, accompanying us home?

Hello moon .

From the *Mary Murray*'s upper deck

the wind is stiff in our faces

Another Spring as warm

ten days earlier

the moon is still out

another year falling across its face so slow-

ly, so flatly the motion of wave as I do

fall back astonished, take my glasses off,

the shore lights

so close

fuzz to myopic eyes naked sting in the wind, the

tide is full, he said, the moon lies fair upon the straits .

Let me tell you, let me tell

you straight, strait and very narrow indeed, encloses

the night encloses all but the bright moon, night does not close

upon the bright

Lights white

or red

mark the

bell buoy's

clang against the dark bay

over it, over . it . Year falls across the bright face of .

Tail of Brooklyn ferry disappears behind

                                      an anchored tanker, fail

              I fail to see and put glasses back on,

I fail

to .

Laughter along the lift of deck

lovers stand at the rail, close on

              From the rail we see

the figures of moondance flicker, see

fireglow from the interior of the

                      island .

The smell of smoke

comes out on the breeze across the lower

                    bay,

to us, ten days later, a year gone,

            burnt across a bright face

that looks like it's been chewed on,

            but will not die .

The quarter-moon glints on the water

nailed,

nailed on the sky

                      Goodbye moon .

            V . 19 . 64

NY 3

for Fee

Man

sits in a rattan chair

staring away to not care, to

wear nothing

get no haircut, to not

see the table behind him

filled with empty glasses

wine bottles

In the eye of his mind, the table

bare . the bottles

of rare wines

all empty

HOW TO GET UP OFF IT

Any mountain climber will tell you
it's a matter of knowing yourself,
your skill . Even the older men,
a world locked in itself, as also
the laws of place escape us, hem us in, in
some forgotten way, as themselves :

"Am I ready for this mountain?"
and they go. Up.

Around 6 of a summer evening
the pigeons are that engaged.
On the east front of the Public Library at 42nd Street

it is a matter of sitting.
On the wall SE of the entrance from 5th Avenue, seven or eight
          stand on a narrow ledge
          and are falling asleep
               or about to, beaks
             turned to the wall, fall
               asleep .

                    Four on the south urn,
                    on the north urn three.

A third of the way up the face, on
the edge of the second ice-field, not
just the rain of pebbles and dirt, but
going flat on your face, falling rocks
flashing off hats, shoulders,
smashing plastic cups in the knapsacks,
the sheer face, the near misses...

             Standing on the north lion, one,
                  on the south lion, two pigeons.
On the rounded edge of the empty fountain, south
side of the steps, one lies down   .   Not all those
against the wall seem asleep, even immobile, but most   .

in some forgotten way
we carry the marks of places all our lives,
a kind of fate   .   her   .   whoever she is,
she swings on his arm and smiles, leans
          toward us
          and smiles .
I acknowledge the greeting somehow and
squeeze Sara's hand at the same time   .   This
world, the double avenue of trees, this
world is locked in itself, a central lawn,
the flower beds empty .

On this west side facing the park,
there are two birds who walk alone, circle
about one another,
puffing and circling slowly. The
game
is for the smaller one to seize the beak of the larger
and pull it down to the stone.

They grapple beaks and bob,
interminably almost. On
one corner of my bench a
girl in tight slacks is writing a long letter to a boyfriend.
She reads his letter over first, then begins her own:
"O God, I can't say it. If I only could" it starts. She also
watches the two pigeons at their beak game, hand across
her breast
resting on her shoulder while
she watches the beak game
and thinks of the next sentence.

A third of the way up, it's a way of knowing yourself, the world
not locked in its place but all that mountain coming down in
pieces on the back, shoulders, I'm flat on my, the arm
covering the face, tick-tick, will I ever get off it? whack!
another rock hits the knapsack, get up and go on?

        The pigeons seem never to tire
        of the game.
        Do any of us?
        Finally they circle and stroll, drop
        down
                toward the lawn,
      stroll off into the sunset together
              sort of .
                    Ro-mance .

or back down again?
Locked in myself   .   her   .   whoever she is .
The way is focused,
the formality of a way into life,
twice, three times attempted .

CONCOMITANTS

fishing in the dark pools of the mind, one finds a

GREEN E-

VENING & THE SKY

        clears,

& the sea flats out & the crickets start

their EVEN-

ING . The

(song)

lights are up,

sun down .

Dishes on the table, one

deep & platter-shaped for, say, home fries, was

my grandmother's, pale yellow, pale resentments

with pale roses

painted on it

Another, a

platter, has a gold rim

on oyster-white 10¢-store china, I

don't even know why it gets to me

(after holding it for hours

finally peeing my pants in

the summer dusk

Exquisite relief of the warmth

trickling beneath short pants

in the summer

("can't see—")

past this green-blue evening by the sea

shore, 30-odd years later .

THE CONCERN

One wonders about the hands and ribcages
of men all over this land

and brackish ponds
& breaking icy surfs

or I do   .
where are you?

I wish I knew one jubilant man, one
completely fulfilled woman.

There are the two places,
there always are

CATHERINE, AT EVENING

Catherine Ledoux

was someone who

I was not permitted to play with

at age 5 .

No explicit sense of her left from the dream, but

the smell of fresh clothes drying

in someone else's backyard

at evening .

FOREIGN POLICY COMMITMENTS OR
YOU GET INTO THE CATAMARAN FIRST, OLD BUDDY

y digamos que, pensamos que, like
it doesn't work, you
talk of the war in Vietnam—only you don't—
dear committee, you talk most about ways
of expressing your rage against it, only
you do not say it is rage, too
timid, baby, you are a beast in a trap,

     fierce but rational

     (maybe they'll let me out?)

     You know they won't

and there's the persistent sense of animal rage, to
strike back, to strike out
at what hurts you, hurts them too, I mean the reality

the children who will grow up to hate us,
the Vietnamese girl blinded and burnt by our napalm and
  still / lives, has lost all her hair, is
  still pregnant
  and will bear the child if we leave any hospitals for them, if
not, whatever ditch or ricefield or building still standing, that
    10 Americans die
that's her only wish

   I wonder why?
   here we are saving Southeast Asia, etc.
   And everyone knows this, every
   one feels it

   Bombs fall and are flowers
   the stamen is the whole village

blossoming, the
wood and tin and flesh flung outward
are petals . Death
is beautiful! Mussolini's son-in-law, what
was his name, Ciano? count Ciano
has described it accurately . The
image is true . That was 1937

How the villages explode under the blossoming bombs!
Lovely! the bodies thrown up like wheat from the threshing flail?
It sure as hell is poetic and this is 1966 and what shall we
do against it?

The dead horse
nibbles
dead grass
in a dead pasture . There
is no green anywhere, horse,
pasture, grass, it's all

b l a c k .

Whatsa matter with you?
Hasn't anyone
ever seen
a black horse?

GETTING A JOB

How can we stand the soup?

How can we love the pope?

How can we put up with the cops?

and we do . . .

But plenty

of Dante

destroys us,

that great light over us

And the light enters the asshole

and the asshole enters the office

and the office records it   .

THE PAIN

A pert maid, a perty maid, a pretty

maid, a

rock maid, a granite maid,

the rent must be paid

I have a gun

We are climbing fences to pay the rent   .

The girls' names

are Dany Farmer, Barbara Former, and Garulous Monroe,

who is silent   .   but, we know

the money is under the counter .

We'll make it

though

all of it sounds automated .

THE ASSASSINATION OF PRESIDENT McKINLEY

Before Trinity Church

on lower Broadway

3:30–3:35 P.M.

while the casket was being lowered into

the grave at Canton, Ohio,

the portals of giant buildings draped in black,

flags flying at half-mast,

the street is jammed dead with people,

maybe half of the men in bowlers and caps

the other half with their heads bared   .   Some

twenty Lex & Columbus Ave. & Broadway trolleys

stopped as far back as the eye can see on a muggy day,

most everyone jamming the windows murmuring or silent

while the bells of Trinity tolled for   5   minutes .

At Jackson Bros., at 66,

the first-floor windows equally draped, the drapers,

black, one of the brothers takes

advantage in the back of the store

of the dead stop, of

the new little typist in accounting, makes

her bend over the great rolls of fabric

in the stockroom, lifts the voluminous skirt, pulls

down the sad white bloomers,

      undoes his fly,

             spits on the end of his cock, &

                 fucks her, the last rite

for the assassinated Mr. McKinley,

            September 19, 1901

Five minutes of hushed silence, the

bells booming and

schluk-schluk, the soppy petals of cunt, the groans, &

Tyley Jackson's yell of come is drowned,   gone

under the final two strokes of Trinity's bell .

FACES 1.

Who in New York in 1965 would have

such incredible taste as to do a little girl's hair

in long skinny skeins of curl *à la*

Shirley Temple, *Little Miss Marker* stage?

The wonderful Puerto Ricans. The

taste so bad, the effect is wondrous

beautiful, and so she is

a brown little waif-wife, 5-yr-old opposite me on a

Lexington Avenue train

in a peppermint red-&-white stripe dress with

some legend needlepointed neatly in across

the bottom of the skirt I can't read

      B E L O   —T O—

                              i t   s a y s .

She pulls it down prim looking at me

reproaching?   Can it be?

        She thinks I'm looking up her dress?

So I do.

        Not very interesting.

It's her eyes that get me : the

severe quality in the reproach

has already faded, re-

             ceded in favor of

                        —migod— friendliness.

A friendly reproach, then, from *Shirle Temple*,

that's fading away, and there's a

look of satisfaction (5 yrs old?)

that makes me wonder what my face looks like .

The part of the skirt she'd tucked between her knees

pops up again—starch, crinoline maybe?

well, it's still not very interesting.

Her father finds something, tho, there's a spot

just above her right knee, bruise, dirt, what's

that?   he asks, she shrugs, he takes his hand away.

The letters visible on the skirt read now :

—LONGS   —TO—

I guess the legend now, it's incredible, he

can't keep his hands off her legs, lays

his slender hand over her knee just as

they rise to exit at Grand Central

Station .   Well, I'm right, the skirt

d o e s   have a crinoline and the message reads finally :

M Y   H E A R T   B E L O N G S   T O   D A D D Y

I ' l l   j u s t   b e t   .   The curls down

the back of her neck are perfect. In

her care not to scuff the patent leather shoes

with their sad shine,

she stumbles a bit at the doors

Goodbye, *Shirle Temple*, goodbye !

which close

all at once .

O, DO THAT MEDIEVAL THING AGAIN, BABY

Love is a weakness, a
sickness, a fear & a terror, and—

     I love I can do that
     and risk
     that evil thing
wherein our own heart go forth from us

NEWSCLIPS 2. (Dec/ 6-7)

     The news keeps squirting in from all over,

     it's like a leak in my head.

The two astronauts in Gemini 7 took a snapshot

of a Polaris missile yesterday,

shot from a nuclear sub parked near the Cape.

Co-pilot Cmdr. James Lovell cried

as the missile broke water:

       "We've got 'er, we've got 'er!

        She's beautiful!"   sitting

          there in his underwear.

Somewhere around the 30th orbit

he had climbed out of his space suit.

The first zippers he unzipped somewhere

around the Canary Islands .   40   minutes

and 11,000 miles later, over Madagascar,

he's gotten down to his longjohns.

"I feel naked," he said, and also

"It's the only way to fly!"

Frank Borman was supposed to

get undressed later,

I never heard what happened.

But what a great idea, a pair

of astronauts

orbiting earth for two full weeks

in their underwear!

What happens when they get horny?

"Hey Jimmy, I see you got a hardon."

"Allright, Frankie, boy, you wanna

do something about it?" And Frank

cuts off the blood pressure telemetry, pulse, re-

spiration, and so forth,

& so far as the Houston Space Center's concerned,

they're dead?

Imagine when they start sending ladies up,

coeducational orbiting, wow,

LOVE AT FIRST FLIGHT   . o, the headlines

and the usual housekeeping chores . . .

Meanwhile,

back at the pad, Gemini

6   is being readied for liftoff

scheduled this Sunday, the 12th.

Walter Shirra and Tom Stafford are to try

to effect a rendezvous with the other two boys.

And in Miami,

Rep. Walter H. Moeller (O.)

an ordained Lutheran minister

and a member of the House Space Committee

on vacation,

protested the launch on Sunday of the spacecraft:

"In these days of crisis," he said,

"we need all the moral and spiritual re-

sources

we can muster."

I'm surprised he didn't complain about the underwear.

Well, I'm about to the end of the broadcast.

High tides for today, Dec/ 7, at Sandy Hook

6:20   A.M. and 6:46 P.M.;   6:33 A.M. and 7:07 P.M. on

the North side of Montauk Point;

at the Battery   6:49 and 7:12   .

Temperatures yesterday were various:

88° and clear in Kingston, Jamaica
84 and cloudy in Acapulco
85 and partly cloudy in San Juan
41° and cloudy in Paris,   59   in Rome
52° and clear in Athens

36 and snow in Moscow
84° and cloudy in Saigon, in Copenhagen
34° and snow;   57 and partly cloudy in
both Cairo and Tunis .

Aldebaran is very bright to the East at sunset,
Altair and Vega in the West at the same
hour   (4:29);
Venus very bright in the West, rising at
7:30 P.M.; Mars reddish and
low in the West an hour earlier.
Again at sunset (4:29)   Jupiter
is very bright to the East, and Saturn
likewise in the Southwest .
And tomorrow, Dec/ 8, the moon is full .

And on Sat., Dec/ 11, the Home Lines
announce a 4 P.M. sailing of the *Oceanic*
from Pier 84 North River, at 44th St.
which is listed in the ship schedules

as   "Cruise to Nowhere."

Don't miss it, boys and girls, and that's

all for tonight.

BLUEGRASS

Field of blue-white

light, sharp

over the bent heads, the instruments

useless in their reflections, all

the questions are wrong,

blue field of arc light, fluorescent, the

answers to them ir-

relevant. Put paper there

and an instrument some where

close, there are

those valleys dark below the darkening mountains,

no word comes .

"Well, writers don't live forever."

"True, but just the same . . ."

The blue park sits in the mind as another place we live,

the sun, perhaps, later south under the blue hills

" . . . it's always going to be a surprise

to me if I don't."

the

knife reflects the light uselessly,

the work is only

what is not done .

ST. MARK'S-IN-THE-BOUWERIE

—Cargo's outbound, the supercargo speaks,

"Reality comes on fast or slow"

One by one, we finish things with gusto

and if we're lucky end up two-by-two

walking along the rim of some

not-yet-extinct

volcano.

David Amram on French horn takes a solo,

a sort of tender pear, *molto largo.*

When there's nothing anyone can do,

      reality

comes on fast or slow.

Cut or hack, plant the avocado;

death is no tornado, it's a crack

that widens,

separates us from ourselves

and things that happened to us years ago,

a kind of seed split open, so will grow

root and leaf, up and down, to air and soil.

What we cannot do, we cannot spoil,

and there is nothing anyone can do.

No anticipation and no love, now;

reality comes on fast or slow,

and fire comes up to meet us as we go.

SEVENTEEN NIGHTS LATER AT McSORLEY'S : 2/10/66

"I know you," he sed,

little man in a tan coat and black hat

at the end of the bar

        "from the hospital," he sed,

    "visiting Reardon, you wuz

    visiting Reardon. I wuz

    in the next bed to him."

        —B-3? I asked.

"B-3," sez he. "Next bed to him,

I seen you."

   —You won't see him again, sez I

  "No?"

      —No. You're well again? Mazeltov.

  "No?"

      —No.

SUNFLOWER ROCK

    "C'mon, get out,

    y'gotta get out," sez Milly,

    "stop sleeping'n get out, I call the cop."

The old man

crumples up his check and drops it onto the sawdust floor.

"Mary," he says, and staggers to his feet and

begins to come on to Mary behind the counter. She

wipes the glass counter and does not meet his eyes,

says, "You'll get out now."

He does, stiffening his body and pushing it back

off the counter with his arms, reels

      lightly toward the door:

         "See ya tomorrow, Mary," and

            something else low.

               "You'll get out," she says.

                  He does.

Milly the waitress is full of plump wrath and righteousness

finding the unpaid, crumpled bill on the floor: "He
comes in, eats, he goes ta sleep,
don't even pay his bill!" Milly
lays the crumpled paper on the counter.
          I suppose there's a place to put it.

"Hey, he's all right, he
just thinks it's a flophouse!" Aunt
Ella joins in, having emerged from the kitchen
       where she is these nights,
          wipes her hands on her apron
            and grins .

              "Sunstroke!" it's Max,
              a customer at the front table,
              "He wuz
              hit in that head widda sunflower!"
              makes the finger-gesture
              to his own head.
He sports a new pair of those half-sized aluminum crutches
crippled open on the chair beside him.

The circles grow from the stone.
Woodie, black dog with a curly tail,
circles back of the counter, out front again.
The Mrs. circles up from the ovens to find out
what the shouting's about . Mary
circles back of the register for someone who does pay .
Aunt Ella circles back to the kitchen,
another order's in .

Struck in the head with a sunflower,
the old man's circle has taken him out the door

into the rain.
Outside,
the night is full of March rain,
That was the joke,
some joke . and the evening traffic uptown .

Soon,
we step into it ourself, stop
to buy a half-pint at the corner
for the cold night, for the pocket.
Already wet, we turn our back to the northwind,
feel the whiskey burn .

RITUAL X. : THE EVENING PAIR OF ALES

EAST OF EDEN
is mountains & desert
until you cross the passes into India   .
It is 3 o'clock in the afternoon or
twenty of 8 at night, depending
which clock you believe .

AND WEST IS WEST
It's where the cups and saucers are,
the plates, the knives and forks .

The turkey sandwich comes alone
or with onions if you like
The old newspaperman always takes his hat off
& lays it atop the cigarette machine;
the younger, so-hip journalist, leaves his on
old-style .

The old man sits down in the corner, puts
   his hat back on. No challenge, but
    it's visible, the beau geste .
    The cigarette
hangs from the side of the younger man's mouth, he's
putting himself on .
   East of Eden is mountains & desert & every
    thing creeps up on you & comes in the night,
     unexpectedly .
when one would least put out his hand
to offer, or to defend .

THE ISLAND

Six men stand at the bar
Seven men sit at the tables
   now eight
    now nine
a sixteenth man in the urinals
Matty behind the bar
George in the back .
Silence there is &   2   conversations
   sometimes   3   .
It is March 9th, 3:30 in the afternoon

The loudest sound in this public room
is the exhaust fan in the east window
   or the cat at my back
    asleep there in the sun
     bleached tabletop, golden
      shimmer of ale .

EZRA'S CONTRIBUTIONS

>   As for the politics
> order, justice, fiscal and otherwise,
> which ended in Dachau and Belsen, i-
> >   deas going into action, etc.,
>
> >   "It's a lonesome day today"
> >   the blues says and
> >   (economists see money as abstract)
> >   "it looks like tomorrow
> >   will be the same damn way."

SAM

My pants wear thin

when the wind blows

—north or south—

I know it   .   Let me

tell you how Rembrandt painted

in his old age   .

THE CROSSING

The stream
piles out of the pile-
up of earth—
we call them mountains—

It
runs west to east
roughly, or
from where it starts in the
pileup of earth, it runs
ESE
      to be very exact.   And
in spring the birds cross it
           heading north   .

Thousands and thousands of birds
heading north cross it heading
north   .
         Singing   .   it makes everyone
        very happy   .   the
stream is reasonably happy by itself
         running ESE
               as it does
      & is basically unaffected
   by all those migrations
of thousands and thousands of birds   .

A MAJOR MANIFESTATION OF THE PROBLEM, IS THE PROBLEM

You appear
here on these slopes
a tired, slim, still-desireable messenger

It has been solitary
among the rocks
these two weeks,   O there've
been people, friends, work,
reasonably cheerful   with vibrations
           If one's
body turns on unexpectedly, one

can always take it for a long walk
       dissipating juices
       strengthening
       (the same in the long run)   muscles .

          A cold shower after a hot works
          miracles in the mind . even
the imagination flakes out and only the eyes come alive
to that register of
small animals, trees, rock, cloud, every
thing outside .

But now the context
changes, tho perhaps
the habit does not .   to
read the sun on the side of Aspen Mountain
as an hour to wake and . turn . and then
to rise fully as whatever man I am
     to you, fully, explicit .
             What is the message?
                       I'm afraid
         the same as usual . I dress,
draw curtains on the window and leave you there
to reconstitute yourself into someone who
may someday love me .   Hard rock
on the radio .
Coffee's lonesome, a delicate
cottonwood seed floats in the open window, lands
in my outstretched hand turns naturally to take it .
Look at it a moment then
crush it against my trousers .
plant it in my thigh, as if that were soil
or any other dirty wholesome thing . rock

     Lonesome's the word for it,

             that sense of it .

       WALK   the mountain

         another hungry animal .

MEASURE THE TAKERS

How the words there

stand for less than it is, is

the hard way to make it, friend.

Try'er, take a shower

dry'er

hair, and aspirin by Bayer

    (briar is truly a pipe

or a kind of hay)

    cali . for . ni . ay

right back where I started

(from) .

How they fill up shirts

    The real question .

BAGGS

KEEP no names that give us not

our death

To roll into it

and stay there warm

The seats of the mountains

    hold the water table close

I want her hands on my back

      though that not be possible

The grey bull codifies what we un-

        able, dis-prove

          chugchug, the jaw of

what softness we rut toward

and the rock of wool pulled short the

mountains stand

under the forks of rivers

The bowman lays it out and keeps us

down

no names

that give us not our death,

o swift current, o buffalo .

MESSAGE TO MICHAEL

      I wish to say
      that a mouth
      lies other
      where than
      where it is
      North—West—

        South of me somewhere

It is invisible

and unattainable

I talk with it always   .

THE GEOLOGIST

The rain falls in fresh gusts

corner of

the pass end of

this mountain town   .   The dogs

trot silent   .   People

cook their suppers

and smoke.

When the peaks rose in the Tertiary, fire

spilled upward under the rain .

The nonexistent liners on this

                    boiling inland sea

                    remind us, they

                    pass in yr/ eyes .

THE SOUNDS

Listen, Death
Beth, see, it's
not so bad . . .
you were the most un
conquerable, he sed, ocean I ever had, speaking to the Atlantic.
The noises in the night are cries for help
and listen to the neat
piping in the night
it's far from men

the paper's torn
and so's the word
the nails have done their
trick. the town
sits in our laps and laps, the neolithic fen
is far from born, the town
is there in the faroff sounds and
morning's rain comes in.

DEPARTURE : THE SOUNDS OF SILENCE

Sirius bright over Smuggler
The Hunter is over the Pass

                /   September almost

5 in the morning, almost . I
hate it, leaving the valley .
Walking thru deserted streets
the air is brisk without wind, no
cars, no
dog barks,
nothing
moves except myself

& the hunting dog over Smuggler
& Orion over the Pass .

MATCHBOOK POEM

        BUT   WHY   do you go to the wall?

        W H Y   d o e s   h e g o t o t h e w a l l ?

        You go to the

wall because

that's where the door is

maybe .

THE SURROGATE

She stole ma hat

     ma hat   .   was in the lounge with ma jacket

The jacket she dint take it, but

                ma hat, she tukkit, clean

                outa the place . she liked

ma hat   .   & went with it to the room & danced,

    DANCED with it, wearin the hat she

                    D A N C E D !

she

danced,   and dint expect I'd cum back ferit   .   ah did .

      Pretended I hadn't figured it out

      talkin with her friend . I'd figured

        she laiked ma hat .

Next mornin, nobuddy up, both of 'em sleepin late .

        "Come in"

          /

            I did, & there it wass,

ma hat

on the bed . she'd bigod

        slept with ma hat!

1967–71

THE GLORIOUS MORNING

/1/

                                      Sun bright on the water, some
                                        small birds over our wake, terns,
/   birds .   The birds turn . fishing
                                            over our wake,
                                 over the sun on the swells

To wake this morning
to wake with a girl in my bed
  a second consecutive morning
            first time in over 40 days and 40 nights
and she thinks I reproach her for having to leave me
in the first hour of light   /
                still virgin   /
                       ah, no .
Virtue unrewarded perhaps, but the pleasure she gives me!
To wake once more
a girl in my bed .   a song about a dancing bear in my head
IT IS ME, I WRITE IT DOWN IN THE AIR !

         Birds on the sea
         sun and clouds

dance of waves in the sunlight
dance of birds in the air
dance of the bear in my head
dance of her quick step across the cabin floor
in the corridor, the dance of mop and pail
I hum:
"I'll taste the things I please"   picking
long soft hairs from my pillow
small cunt hairs from my bed
so that cabin boy from the song, now mopping the gangways, will
have no stories to retail after he makes the bunk   /   my head
hums a jumble of tendernesses for what this lovely head

has given me .

And for all those more
glorious mornings
in the mind .

Pas du succès   toute la nuite

so we sleep

sleep   .

In the morning,
we do something fairly sensible, very
homely even, we go and have breakfast

together .

ACROSS   THE   TABLE,   eyes

at meeting   .

Then,
after breakfast go
once more to the upper deck :
stand in the sun for a bit
ignoring the others   .

THE   SUN !

Return to the cabin finally,
and there, it does happen,

it does   .   & it does
& goes on happening for a long time, the

other morning
.
now .

<u>3</u>/

The city stands about us
& friends .
Toward the east after supper .

She sd/ "Yeah?"
I sd/ "Yeah."

AND IT WAS TRUE !

Cuntsmell everywhere, it
took me hours to wash, I didn't want to.
We even got to sleep early,
slept enormously.

18, rue de la Harpe
Hôtel de Levant, le vent

n'est pas ici, c'est bien nous
NOUS SOMMES ICI,   Joan, what
time is it now, three?

We even got to sleep early .
Our cool hands .

/4/

Sipping calvados in the Café des Invalides
                    after morning coffee .
          Rain drips from the eaves,
                              leaves fall .
The gutters are up and running
                              brimfull .
September .   o Christ, Paris .   tout à fait normal .

                    Feuilles des marroniers
          to be swept up when it stops
          maybe next month sometime .

And the place Dauphine-en-l'Isle
is all fucked up by construction
between the Hôtel Henri IV
& the Palais de Justice .

And it falls and falls forever .
And looks as if the rest of these glorious mornings
                    are going to be wet as hell .

                    from JOURNAL ENTRIES, September 1967 .

UNCHARTED

Sun is that
rare in Paris, I
          almost swim in it

the day accomplishes itself with its
          small failures & annoyances

Its pleasures mount gently toward evening
walking many strange streets toward

home, it were . no map, o Joan!
Let me come before you a triumph and
          a happy man!

JOURNAL . 7 XI 67 ff

Green shoes
black umbrella
stands on her good legs outside the school for an hour .
Checks her watch & vistas of
doorways, corners   .   People pass

          Alas, neither she nor he.
He's in Memphis and lord only knows where she is .   The
rainfall, the umbrella, the watch, the green shoes,
the green rainbow, the umbra, watch the shoes, they
move, see?

198

Kiss / kiss!   A

& I do   miss   B L U E S

you .

Let me be where

that next

other glorious morning

     will be

& not in the mind either, babe,

not never no more in the mind

babe, not never no more in the mind .

Cold birds out the window trying to sing

Sweep of the sea   .   moving water   .   much further awa?

     I got rights

     to be blue, noo?

Who are we?

Let us see

     a gull   and a porpoise

¿cómo no?

     better

than any marriage I have had or

     could think of .

"I've been fixin a hole where the rain comes in"

& below is 17th Street, Nashville, the

cross-thru below Fisk campus

                    where is

LIQUOR STOREs, BARs, CLEANERS, numerous BARBER SHOPs,

burger joints, a movie, & even a gas station, ES-

SO es . y no es . si-saw . So.

Off they go, back to Memphis,

                    tank full of gas and a

                    pocketful of rye .

The rest of this town is located else-where

     DOWN-TOWN . and is scary as shit

mean white mouths and steel eyes out

gunning for my beard and long hair and tight jeans

The eyes say it loud and hard   NIGGUHLOVUH!   and

I surely am, all the beautiful faces I see downtown

are black .   a pleasure to take bus back

                    to the ghetto, that's where it is, Morton .

                    I am a nun here for days

                         soon shortened.

Where were all they

     &

it was not me .   When it was

I was there.

"How is you spell PO-EMS, man?

            ▱

If you're looking

    for where it is where

    it really is, never

    choose no road   .   What

    ever road you take will

    tell you, make you go

        take you

            to

where

it

is

REALLY.   ▱

                    GIVE ME LIBRIUM or

                    GIVE ME METH—

among graffitti on sculpture, center of Astor Place
between the Cooper Union buildings, Nov. 10, 1967

GIN

Clear objects, the
clear objections   .   The gulls
float thru the yard   .   The wall-

paper is stained, sections are
pure Cretan linear-B .

                I fled New York somehow,
                it's all hers now . And cold .

Amsterdam is full of sun, it falls
aslant ten buildings in the next street
I can see from my window—the Dutch
        believe in large windows, it
is exactly the width of the room, a long narrow
Van Gogh-room, even the skinny bed
        in the right position .
Except the canal is at the front of the ho-tel,
so the room faces
what I wd/ call
the wrong direction.

                Black roofs and red roofs   .   Tile.
                While,
blackbirds in the shadowed backyard
hop about thru bright yellow leaves, or
flap between the lower branches .

An enormous gull just swooped thru the yards
        leisure-ly .

The canal at the front of the ho-tel,
go to it   .   Read the cards.

                Even with sunlight, I am lightly depressed .
                Foto, September 18, the boat-train
                Le Havre to Paris   .   Joan confronts
                the French landscape   .   the gold locket,

her toothmarks in it . Good, tight
lens on that camera.   Blue
dress, blue landscape blurred

    O shit,
    I left my heart in the 7th arrondissement
    a good bit South of here, apparently.

    Forget it. I've left my heart everywhere,
    walk around collecting bits and shards .

Gil, how do you keep
such a unified vision of your own
       lives   /   & parts?

I take trains   /   or planes

      boats   /   or goats

Gull flies thru the backyard one way
crosses pigeon flying thru the other   .   Damn,

this gin is good!

BIRDS / AMSTERDAM

Flurry of fat sparrows hits the fence
top near the Oude Turfmarkt, whence

       look very surprised
       to have made it
       look around

10 notes   2 chords
I try to sightread
the melody   /   too fast, they've gone

In the tiny square NW side of the
Leidseplein   where is a carpark   the
trees are full of grackles   .   Taxi
stand   .   taxidriver, no fare, stops
briefly, gets out, slams his door,
walks to the nearest (one of the youngest) trees
& kicks it
                        hard & high   .   the sky
is blackened   .   the ears attacked

        The driver smiles
        The big birds circle
        drift & land again
He gets back in the car and drives off.
Still smiling

At the Dam by Moses Aaronstraat
the Sunday afternoon is filled with
solid citizens, their overcoated arms, shoulders
loaded with pigeons doing the neck-ring peck
:   little girls with their hands full
The pigeons cluster & waddle & fly
in packs, circle up to the roofs & back
& keep the air full of wings   .   to be fed

Prinsengracht   .   Herengracht   .   Singelgracht
    families   .   flocks   /   quack
        it's ducks swimming along leaving
        delicate wakes along the quiet canals
        Well, not so quiet   .   QUACK   .

Sarphatipark   /   Vondelpark
a few songbirds   (more grackles,
more sparrows) .   Amsterdamsebos
more of the same plus some few
swans, mean-beaked, very white, plus

EVERYWHERE
my gulls

above rooftops, on them,
into backyards, over canals
bridges, parks & markets,
business streets, Centraal Station,
the Amstel, the Singel, Rokin,
Osdorp & Slotermeer, Entrepôtdok,
Het ij, Dijksgracht, Ertshaven

Mostly the birdsound
in this town is harsh
&   in/over everywhere
my gulls
hustle food

big & tough or
small & compact
they make it

tho the Paleis on the Dam
belongs to the pigeons

But, I'd heard all that about storks
nesting in chimneys .   did not see any storks
Where are the storks?

Nov. 18-20, 1967
Amsterdam

PARIS, AND NOT SPRING EITHER

The young man

in the next booth

in the café

is waiting for

while he studies

& looks at me

occasionally while I

translate & wait for

We exchange

glances, shy &

His girl arrives first .   I feel
her presence over my right shoulder
before he sees her I see her
She is blond and very pretty

Mine is brunette

& has not arrived yet

He & I both

smile . this city.

MUSÉE DES AUGUSTINS : TOULOUSE

KARTHA
ginian lamps, shaped
like shells to fit the hand—2 flames—
one lifting at each end of that beautiful curve, did they
      join?   Lovers' lamps .

     put in some oil and see

& Etruscan cups, five/six
centuries before that god came down, all
               jet-black
               with big ears
               held like a dipper,
    probably dipped in the jar—spill
a bit onto the floor first, for the gods

The guards
who'd confiscated my camera stayed
down by the *caisse* at the entrance
so I touched all the statues of Venus
cunt, belly and breasts
All those of Bacchus and Hercules
I tickled under the balls, just to be sure

& Lucius Verus   (161-169 A.D.)
looked just like Robert David   .   I passed
a pleasant hour with the goddess, the gods   .

Toulouse, November 1967

VALENCIA : WINTER

Sunrise now
abt/   8:15 every morning
Light starts coming over before that

     It's such a drag to wake up in the dark,
      and I do .

No one to turn to, I
may read for a bit, turn the heater on, the
    light off, try
    sleep another hour
     or two

  The light
  when it does come
  is timeless

Check the sky & eat an orange .
then make coffee .

FOG

My hands sit there
turned on my knees, in-
ward and soft, a few
wrinkles along the back, I stretch them out .
They hold a white
cigarette, and are brown .

        Gulls balance
        swing in pairs up
        thru this weather .

Thunderstorm
beats against the windows, 8 or 9
lines of surf breaking   . whap .
whitecaps on the sea, color
muddy green today, far as I can
see, which isn't that far .

Lightning strikes again
so many ways, parallel to the waves this time
I hardly notice the thunder, tho it was loud
The hands are
brown, I tell you .   fog .

THE INGESTATION : OR TAKING IT ALL IN

I try to, per-
haps I try too hard
to select it, to choose, o I CANNOT!
it cannot be deliberate, you don't choose

YOU JUST LOVE, THAT'S ALL

it is a force   .   fierce,

she   .   whoever she is   .   is

unavoidable

The openings are screwed up tight

and I bring her here

just to know

   where she is

   I am   .

   The loathly lady tells

   Arthur, middle of that wood, what

   all women want most : 'Their own way'

   That is very true

The same is true of men, also.

"He had his way with her"

no idle expression

   You strike the earth hard

   & enter it, finally,

     & forever .

THE NET OF PLACE

Hawk turns into the sun

over the sea, wings red, the

turn upward . mountain behind me

I have left those intricate mountains

My face now to the simple Mediterranean . flat .

small boats . gulls . the blue

Old hawk
is still there tho, as
there are foxes on these barren mountains   .
      Old man in a beret, 62 perhaps, came
      into the village bar the other day
      —2 skins and one fox unskinned—

      "You hunted these down?"

      "I hunted them. They
      come in closer in winter, seeking food,
      there isn't much up there—"

Rocky headland down into the Gulf of Valencia .
My windows face North . He was a hawk

I turn back to the Rockies, to the
valley swinging East, Glenwood to Aspen, up
the pass, it is darkest night the hour before dawn,
Orion, old Hunter, with whom
I may never make peace again, swings
just over the horizon at 5 o'clock
as I walk . The mountains fade into light

Being together there was never enuf,—it was
"my thing" Nothing of importance (the reach)
was ever said . I turn
& say farewell to the valley, those hills   .
A physical part of wellbeing's been spent &
left there—Goodbye mountains   .   valley,
all. Never
to be there again . Never.

It is
an intricate dance
to turn & say goodbye
to the hills we live in the presence of .
When mind dies of its time
it is not the place goes away .

    Now, the hawk turns in the sun, circles
    over the sea .
            Defines me .
    Still the stars show thru   .

Orion in winter rises early,
summer late . dark before

          dawn during August
          during which day, the
          sun shines on everything.

               Defines it .
           Shadows I do not see.

I rise early
in every season.

    The act defines me,
    even if it is not my act .

          Hawk circles over the sea .

               My act .

Saying goodbye, finally .
Being here is not enuf, tho
I make myself part of what is real.   Recognize me

standing in that valley, taking only the embraces of friends, taking
only my farewell . with me

> Stone from my mountains .
> Your words are mine, at the end.

HOW TO ENJOY FISHING BOATS

Sit on the terrace
& look
at them, inshore tonite,
across all that greying
blue .
hear (chug) . count
the boats

Ee/ush,
waves coming in   (don't count)
the beach below, low sound, then two
bikes downhill
from the construction site
One is a motorbike, its tires
smooth on the roadway, its weight, no
motor on, the other, motorless, clanks
lightly
at every unevenness

> Later a car comes down,
> a 600, the foreman's a
> likely guess, it chugs . The

lighthouse goes on,

opens its eye to come to us all,

a half hour later now

than when I arrived on this coast a month ago .

February : the moon two days off full, high

already in the eastern sky . My

girl leaves the room

because she thinks I am working &

              a workingman shd/ be alone

              with his mind,

                    whatever that is .

RITUAL XVI. IT TAKES AN HOUR

Clear empty days like this

            one after the other. I sit

:sun on the balcony, eat an orange

save the pits, set them in

the sun to dry

           Later, I eat

from the piles of paper anywhichway

on the table, old manuscripts, letters, money,

contracts, other men's poems, feed

questions & answers into my typewriter

    for hours before you ask me,

                "Are you hungry?"

You take a long time in the bathroom

always,

gently relieving yourself, then

that long personal

hot water ritual, you stretch

under the shower, torso & limbs for what?

   (seems to me, curious glance at the closed door)

the better part of an hour before the rush of water stops .

stretching again to towel, pat & rub yr skin (I've caught you at

nearly every part of the ritual but

   've never seen it wholl-y, god,

   I'd like to!

     After that,

the face must be prepared, the care

that attends the eyelids,

the mouth, damned good thing we're in the south,

   wear out the mirror, what

    for? me? the

      waiter at the ho-tel? the

       busdriver? and we

have to run finally to make the bus . The bathroom

takes too long . but

I love the suspense .

To watch you walk out, preening

just slightly, a happy smile you

ask me, "Are you hungry?"   while I know

who it is informs my morning, rises, fills my day .

walks round this hillside, bath around herself .

feeds me .

FROM THE JOURNALS; MARCH 1968 : News of Che's death & other political musings, Spanish newspapers being somewhat slow to report certain events.

Plaza de Portal de Elche
in Alicante, wet
from last night's rain .
I had the news in Paris, mid-October, sitting
in a café with Joan, picked up a leftover newspaper
from the next chair, refolded it to the frontpage.
The news is still with me .

It's eight in the morning   .   This square carries an
unintentional message in
its ancient name made new   .

Coffee and *ensaimadas* at
the kiosk set low center
amid the gandules and palmeras
"*Grande como el grande, no ande.*"
¿*Que quieres?*   this early, this late,   2
taxis only on the plaza now . "*Una sombra y
dos ensaimadas,*" instead of
"*La revolución, señor, y dos ensaimadas.*"

¿Por favor?"

Young man stops on one corner at a
shop mirror to
squeeze a pimple or two on his way to work;
looks vacantly at the white
blood-flecked excresence on the
thumb and middle finger of his left hand,
checks the mirror again,

                the hope of Spain .

          By 8:15 there are   4   taxis on
          the side of the square toward the port,
               2   on the lateral and   5
         'minitaxis' on the side toward town .
     The second coffee, this time black, with coñac,
goes down more easily .

[Back at the *pensión*, another quality of certain Spanish newspapers grows
to be of prime importance.]

Stockingfooted down
the tiled & whitewashed
narrow hall, its full
length .

The light works, so
     sit & read :
On the something 28th,
South Yemen tossed out   30   British
     military hired a year ago when
          Yemen became independent .

Foreign Office sends a stiff note—the
Yemenites reply (politely)
that they're saving money .

And an outfit called   RUTHERFORD ESPAÑOLA, S.A., at
    14, General Goded,
                               in Madrid, will
build you a swimming pool shaped like your kidney
out of stone and tile   .   The
rectangles of paper are neatly
torn   .   I tear mine once more
    lengthwise, while thinking
of all the smug accountants in Yemen,
    how polite they are,
and the   30   British advisors
    out of a cushy job

                    while I slowly & carefully
                    wipe   .   Paper's a bit
                    on the slick side .

                    Alicante, March 8, 1968

CUTTING THE MUSTARD

The world and ourselves pass away

We go on

    and enter the dance .

What other chances are there

we could think of as

      already prepared?

THE PROBABILITY

On that not-so-bleak hillside, rocky tho, there's

a bird out there singing a goddamned rondelay

there's a bird out there

also broken bottles, tiles, bricks, trash

flowers (purple, yellow & white) many iris

thorns and rosemary

The hillside is mainly a gray-green, the sea

a bluer green, goes crash below,

repeatedly,

crash   .

      A goddamned rondelay   I think

      she must have built a nest out

      there   .   crash

HALFWAY DOWN THE COAST

What we do
is what we can
do   can
give . the tenderness

CAUGHT GIVING AWAY LOVE

The laying on of an arm
gentle insistence of the hand

The sea insists
on coming to a beach
someplace

The sound is a constant offering
The hurt is suffering
the same things   .   again

I have   19   shirts in the drawer
I could give them all away & have   38
It's a big drawer of
things

And love?   What is that
many-faceted mother?

THE TRADE

Young and as ancient as Spring

the words came sweet, the

tavern owner's wife singing

over the ironing .

Falling silver on our heads

bent over wine . the glasses

clear and golden

RITUAL XVII. IT TAKES AN HOUR

Money seems to avoid me in
some mysterious way

                    so,
                what else should I do, waiting
                for my check to be cashed, but
use a large Hispano-Olivetti and its outsized carriage
sitting in the middle of the floor

First, tho, they
recognized me from similar occasions, the
check had some kind of stamp across its face, and they
said I had to open an account   .
                        OKay,
so I agreed I would open an account if I had to, why not?
Then draw out most of the money, right?

I had the account almost open, all those
questions & answers & signatures, I was even
enjoying it, the
chica filling out the forms filled out a
pretty tight sweater herself, good
legs and lovely breasts resting lightly
            on the desk as she bent
                her forms
                    to those forms   .   Then,
this damned vicepresident comes back to tell me he'd
got permission to pay me cash, I tried to look grateful

So she tore up all that paper and I had to
settle for a nice smile and the bust measurement instead of a
good, solid banking relationship   .

But they weren't thru with me yet:
Had to sign it twice myself (*por
motivo de turismo*, that horror), then
the vicepresident, then a clerk, then
another official of some sort, the whole
damned check is covered with signatures, passport number,
addresses, verifications

        : then I wait

           some more .

The authorization arrives back .   even then, the
window of *Varios Pagos* takes 3   people ahead of me.

So I sit and write the first poem I've ever written in a bank .

It IS a lovely typewriter, and a handsome type .   perhaps
I should come here to write

        all my poems .

                    Barcelona, May 1968

ONE FOR SARA

Making a career of the carretera, to

sit looking at mountains, not that

distant, behind which

the sun has just gone .

I eat a piece of salami with some cheese,

everything goes down . wonder

at the cat's yammering at flies .

And your final silence,

that hammer .

A SHORT, COLORFUL RIOT POEM FOR LEE MERRILL BYRD

Blue
bottles are blue, green
glass is green .
The West tastes like the North
The South tastes like blood and shit
and magnolia .
I think I can stand it

It is the strength in the arms
you feel
if you lift it

      Europe even worse than the States
      the price of kleenex, *boucliers*
      and tear gas
      paving stones and fire
      the same clubs

Cream no longer rises to the top, the
perfection of the centrifuge .
A brown unglazed jar.
The flowers are white
with centers green and yella
how you, fella . the stone
and broken fingernails, it
is the strength you feel
back and arms
when you lift it, *mes copains*

IF you lift it .
The blottolub,
    the cremaris .

THE TOUCH

    The windows
    are never wide enuf .

Calle del Vidrio, Barcelona, is
off Fernando, toward the Plaza Real;
short, tight, narrow, &
    leads toward the palmtrees

The corner bar to the left is
three to five pesetas cheaper than
the one to the right
    as you enter, plenty of
sky, trees, a fountain, the
    arcades sit over each side we
sit with gambas, cervezas, dis-   MARISCAS
cuss my sis-   PERCEBES
ter's imminent   ALMEJAS VIVAS
arrival, I face   CENTOLLOS
the walls, cannot see   Y
the palmtrees behind me   GAMBAS
                                  ALAJILLO
      BEBA COCA COLA   SEPIA
                                  PULPITO

      BAR FARAON

                it says

A quieter day
than yesterday
at the Glorieta, we
sat at the old man's tables in the
back, yesterday, asked
where he was, vacation?
      —No, the other waiter says, he's
dead, came into work on a Thursday
didn't come Friday or Saturday,
Saturday died.

An incredible sadness .
You do not have to know these people's
      names to love them, the way
          the old man moved
          among the tables, an
          organized waddle that
cared for so many so quickly, the new
young man works the same station like
a beheaded chicken, no cool to lose, he
whips it out, everything very organized, but
      it doesn't make the same
          coherence.   Our friend
's tables are full in front so we
             speak only
when he has time   .   None of us
knows anybody else's name .

What was he called, the old man?
A gentleness and efficient waddling is
      dead now. We do
      not need to know
      their names to recognize

a pleasure in feeding people well,

      that rare intimacy, how

miss someone whose name you've never known?

We do not need to know their names, they

minister to us for tips and love they

give is given back   .   The old man

worked the back—four tables only

in the front—sometimes five, it

depended on how heavy the clientele

was that day .   Today, we

take the full *cubierta* the first time .

Again   .   The *viejo* lost to time .

We never know one another's names, tho

we touched each time .

      I'd come back to Barcelona again

      he'd come and touch my shoulder, even

      if I were not at his tables . a greeting . We

do not need to know

anybody's name

to love them.

THE SAIGNON SUITE

THE   SLOPE

Looking up the hill

toward the town, thinking:

the mailman,

telephone call to be made, the
garbage .

BEFORE LUNCH

Cortázar in shorts, that length
stretched along the walk a fair piece,
in the sun   .   in an hour
un apéritif!

THE   DUMP

As you put it
in, over the high fence-boards
one lower edge of the village, the cats
leap out   !!   disappear
in several directions   .   wait   .
watch you .

SUPPER OUTSIDE

The buzz of wasps be now
over the plates on the table
under the fruit trees .

FROM THE NOVEMBER JOURNAL : FIRE

The end of a distance come
so early in the morning
      where the eye stops,
                flames

running O their tongues up thru
     along the rooftree of
         down the coping of
              that church in Harlem .

D R I V I N G   R A I N

Wind driving a winter rain and fire, O
the twigs stripping outside the classroom window
we watch sexy

ANYthing
     vegetable, tall and branched
         yellow, the fire
         yellow, the leaves
         yellow, the girl's blouse
grey, the slacks
grey, the day outside
grey, smoke rising pierced by flames

     turning blue to red to yellow
        Which leads to a discussion of
the personal character of firemen and cops, not
altogether complimentary
     but granting courage   .   A Harlem precinct
     hd/bn firebombed earlier that morning .
Where the eye stops
smoke and flames thru the hill's trees, their
branches stripping . burning the whipping rain
       inscrutable cracks . Whaddya hear?
     The blindman singing on the uptown train
coins in the enamelled metal cup clink

She sits back in the desk no longer thinking
    a dreamy look on her face :
        "It is so pretty," she sez .
Her yellow blouse sighs up and down
The rain strips the branches, drives the
           fire across the church roof
               where the eyes stop.

           /:/

Smoke floats
        in its layers upon
           the room's air   .   has
             nowhere to go . floats
MALIK is king . King is dead of assassin's bullet
Malik is dead of assassin's bullet
Three Kennedys down and one to go .
Dallas is in Texas
California one might have suspected
and Memphis is on the river
and the Audubon Ballroom at 166th Street
belongs to the CIA under prior contract .

        Two cats move in the sunlight
        stream thru the window
        wash, kiss, wrestle, play
        under the smokehaze . they
        are black cats . Yoruba, what
does Oshūn mean? Ouan Jin, or the
        man of education?

Feet raised in sunlight
against the other's face

King dead

Malcolm dead

who   will   be   the   next   to   go?

Ted?

And then she married Onassis,

a prescient woman, to the

Eastern Mediterranean, this time .

You have to transport the stuff

He has the boats . He passes .

My friend, Economou, a medievalist

and poet, owns the most spec-

tacular Afro I've ever seen . The

people pass him in the street and speak to him,

"Hello, brother." He refuses to pass.

But Onassis?

and Jack the Cowgirl?

They pass everywhere, it

is a conspiracy between

East and West .   what

did you think Bouvier meant?

The sunlight goes .

It is a clear light from the South

smogged in .   The cats sit

and wash themselves

in the window,

look out .

What did you think Bouvier meant?

Gassir's lute

The light

shining on Oshūn's face

is not easy to behold . to be held .

Do you think you can put your hat on your head

and walk away with him?   Down that hill?
      But Haarlem is a Dutch name
      and the Dutch have forgotten us .   Deutsch?
The destroyer?   What did you think Oshūn meant?
Ogun,
Yoruba is his tribe
"the six powers of light"
The sunlight across the window, Hooo
Dierra, Agada, Ganna, Silla, Hooo Fassa!
         Wagadu the legendary city of the Fasa .
The epic *Dausi* goes back to   500   perhaps, B.C., at
          which time Homer .   The
remnant of that tribe, mostly Muslim, holds
two desert oases .   Tichit and Walatu .   The blood
of seven of his sons
     dripped
over his shoulder
onto his lute
to feed the song .
       or John?

   "I dig

   talking to a black man   who

   thinks of a white man

   as just another kind of black man."

OR vice versa,

OR thank you, Leo Frobenius

       —to feed the song .

Elaine calls me at 3 A.M. from Toronto. I come up out of a
deep dream, furious. No one else calls me at three in the
morning. I've been sick for two days now. I yell at her and
wish her a happy birthday. Nothing is such a pain in the ass as
being loved where one does not love : it is
an humiliation for both parties
Elaine is just such a pain in the ass. She says
we are married in her dream. I must say she has better dreams
than I do. I'm dreaming of an absolutely natural hair, a single,
intricately curled, long, brown hair in a tiny plastic container
you can see thru like a fuse, loose at both ends, beautifully

involuted and fine. This is an absolutely indispensable item in
a list of objects which must be collected, this wild hair in its
artificial little glass tomb, carefully random, carefully
natural. An absolute fake essential to the collection, essential
for a correct life.

The Ft. Moultrie flag on a recent 6¢ stamp
is the word   LIBERTY   toward the bottom
across a ground of dark blue, and in the upper lefthand corner,
the last quarter of a waning moon .   PIE IN THE SKY .
Ft. Moultrie is in Charlestown, South Carolina .

The black cat comes over and stages a sit-in directly on the note-
book in which one is trying to write a poem .
It is not that she does not know, but will not
confront you eye to eye, sits and looks in another direction
—on your papers.   *And* purrs.

    All right, Elaine, get off my back.

I pick the cat up and put her down on the floor
    & go on.
        And it doesn't stop.   None of it
stops, ever, it needs that wild hair in its
        plastic container, the essential image . So .

I stay up until dawn
        reading Philip Whalen's first book
    which after all these years still turns me on .

"YOU GOIN'TA TELL ME I
    HAFTO GIVE UP
        MAH *P I E C E ?* "

THE TREES

Leaves on the branches
At the end of branches twigs
carrying everything
brushing against each other
reaching toward everything
touching everything   .   The air.

Nov. 1968

[UNTITLED]

There is an irregular movement of the light and

                                         all things are changed
                                         new and old
                                         past & not yet born
                                         enter it
                                         as one

Cannot keep my heart
as bright
as this spring is

                            Lady Godiva on a chopped hog
                            makes it new

Muscles bend it
to the face to
face   .   no turning now, the very way of knowing,
                                       renewing

"I want her hands on my back

                          tho that not be possible"

has been a blue flowering plant of mine,

the most of a year now.

Limonium commune californicum

woody root (that's mine!)   leaves obovate-
to oblong-spatulate, obtuse,
or sometimes retuse, tapering
below into a rather long petiole, 4-9 inches long;
calyx lobes membranous at tip, I'm hip,

corolla violet-purple

a deeper shade of
blue, the closer
I git   to   limonium commune californication

⟋+⟋‾

Eastern window, so
sun on my eye brings
me upright in bed, 7 AM
or so   .   I go

to the phone when it rings
petals of fire =
ize the positions .

"Salt marshes and sea beaches
along the coast, Los
Angeles County to Humboldt County,
July to December"

Jepson sez.

Tho April only
by noon, let us see, what we
can bring to
blossom here this city by the Bay, or
once more, Saxifrage, flowers perfect,
perigynous, usually white, often red,

never blue .

"Seed with endosperm"

Jepson sez.

Olé!

      an irregular movement of the light

               and all things

               move beneath it and

                       are changed .

THE GHOST OF EN RAIMBAUT VISITS LES BAUX

                    Raimbaut de Vaqueiras, son of a poor knight
                    of Provençe, was reported to be the lover of
                    madompna Biatrix, daughter of the marquis
                    Boniface of Montferrat. He was joglar, trobador,
                    & warrior, and flourished in the courts of
                    Provençe and Italy around the middle and late
                    parts of the 12th C. Guillem des Baux, prince
                    of Orange, was one of his first patrons.

My lady Biatrix, Bel Cavalier,

you walked these high stone walls

with this poor sonofa

               mad knight

hand in hand

and laughed .

"That stairway there," you pointed, "brown-eyes."

               The top of all beauty

               and a sword of price .

We bested one another in that joust,

you giving more than you could have promised .

And the stories went out and around .

Roses grew by the walls

                 thorns there, too :

the marquis your father's visit too short for us .

The walls now are full of rooks

the ruins of this high place

where hawks nested .

                   We have walked the valleys al-so.

                   Montferrat later, but

                   first Les Baux .

AGAINST THE SILENCE OF STAIRCASES

Scrap .

whatwe bindoin' all week   .   Blow

all of it up   .   out   .

                   down? what

do those steps mean, worn as they are by

centuries of walking up and down

them, literal *u*'s in the center of them   .   I

ask you, what does my 2nd wife's ass, (fo / to)

pinned to the wall of my workroom, great

generous curves either cheek, rosebush

of hair centering the photograph, the white shirt,

arm fallen over in speechless relaxation,

               mean to you?   Means to me

sleep   .   curling against it   .   seen

               much too often   .   Now

the   S U N   shines outside, first today, the rain and

grey gone from the streets   .

               Man rides a bicycle

up Hall Place, a drunk crosses on 6th St. totters east, the

S T O P   sign lays its white lettering up against

permanent red   .   We

can never go away   .

               Don't never

               go away   .   Not

               even in yr/ head .

PHOTOSYNTHESIS I.

Surrender the grass! Let

all those things grow we have

          so cut back

          all these years .

The crackling of ice in the glass as it

       melts   .   Our kilts but

       cover our asses   .   Tears

       upon the words

ask only other roundness to

encompass with our belly buttons in

a likely juxtaposition .

                Let the old hat roll . Charles

                holds a pipe between his big

easy fists, scarf hangs unevenly in the sun, ankles

crossed, knees wide   .   The glass of pastis

Julio holds to his mouth reflects light

vertically up his nose, the back of his head

       faces southwest   .   We are apt to

       look upon the stairway as tho the steps were

known . 700 years agone ,   Allen's glasses gleam . Gary

holds a hollow knuckle ball between the fingers of his left

hand   .   Ez's eye fixes the machine from under his neat

Alpine hat, the clean raincoat   .   fierce & friendly to

the moustache bristle, beard-jut, but the eye questions

the other end of this gondola, where do the steps lead?

The oarsman ferries him across to

ward a death with windows, romanesque windows flank the

oarsman's ass with balconies   .   The oarsman's headless .

238

Seated beside her man in the *traghetto*, Olga,

gloved and umbrellaed, speaks sensibly

        of the appointment . It is

the Grand Canale after all, and not the Styx .

I take pix

      that auger in, or down upon, or up

      the steps . That cold spring

        was plenty hot enuf,

an old anger evaporated . Her hand cups, touches the

flowers from underneath .

The unexpected kindness of the waters, all

of it fated, the

beauty of the old . of the young .

All of it sung .

                        VII. 70

OCTOBER JOURNAL : 1970

              6 A.M.
              and it's still dark
              on a fall morning

                in October,
                  you goober, you
              keep coming back like the Kelly
              in November, I sed you

              NO-VEMB-ER

        Sunrise is 7:18

The seven moons I can see from this window are

streetlights on campus

The black road is white

           under their light   .   Drops of

           yesterday's rain on the fallen leaves

shine like there are spiders under those leaves, wasps and bees

                  as well . hide there .

                  They hibernate?

                    O bears!

On warm days, bees, wasps, hover over clots of leaves seeking entrance,

or move among the needles

        on branches high in the spruce outside the

           upstairs bedroom window

find, however impossibly, some way in

between the window and screen,

           clenched on the sill   .   die there .

Winter move (ing)   in

My hand creaks

I put the milk back in the icebox

They die there clenched on the sill .

Joan and the boy still sleep away upstairs

Hemlock out the window moves in the light wind

Smoke a cigarette in the dawn-dark .

    talk to myself .

        unheard . unseen .

    I look out the window at seven moons

                              (till night is gone

                              till dawn come)

                    * * * * * * * *

1/5 gal. Virgin Island rum, Old Boston
1 qt. straight bourbon whiskey, Mattlingly & Moore (Lawrenceburg, Indiana)
1/5 gal. tequila, product of Mexico, the Matador Distilling Co, Hartford, Conn.
                              and Menlo Park, California
½ qt. left of John Begg Blue Cap scotch, fr/ the Royal Lochnager Distillery,
                    Balmoral (they ship it from Glasgow, Scotland, U.K.)
enuf Terry Brandy (Fernando A. de Terry, est. 1883) fr/ Puerto de
                    Santa Maria (coñac de Xerez)
and 2 fingers left of Pernod

                    The contents of my liquor cabinet   10   days before
                    you arrive. Vodka's in the refrigerator along with
                    sangria and sweet vermouth de Torino. The California
                    wines are down and cooling. Be welcome.

                    * * * * * * * * * *

Throw this one on your coordinates:

        28 west out of Kingston across
        the Catskill Forest Preserve to   Margaretville

        30 skinnying SW along (and across) the Pepacton Reservoir, a
        dammed sector of the Delaware River (eastern branch)
        down past Shinhopple and Harvard, connecting with Rte. 17
                                        at Eastbranch

        17 west, just before Binghamton catch Interstate 81 north.

The first exit that will jolt you says McGRAW-CORTLAND.

Don't let it tempt you; take the 2nd one, it say

just   CORTLAND .   end of the ramp   STOP sign:

turn left, under the highway to the first light   (2-3

gas stations & a Holiday Inn)   :   turn right

down Clinton into town.

Two more lights will stop you at Main St. (where Clinton ends his upriver

run—but sail on, captain, my brother) right on: the street

changes name to Groton Avenue. Second light on Groton, hard

by a hamburger stand called Hardee's, steep left up the hill

on Graham two long blocks

(the college will lie on yr/ right
dorms to your left)
to

Prospect & a STOP sign.

Pause carefully, edge, noting especially

the hill coming up fr/ yr/ left

(no STOP sign there), then:

a slate-grey shingled corner house, facing Calvert (extension of Graham)
Cape-Cod roof;
then an awkward, more modern contrivance, aqua & white with a carport,
very slow:
the white-porched #60 is where we is, the driveways a foot apart. With
luck you'll see the VW wain therein, dark green, shaming the maples.

The leaves will be on the ground, brother, and the branches bare, but

the welcome warm.

* * * * * * * * * * * * * * * * * * *

Alternate route: Kingston, thruway to Catskill; 23 west skimming north end
of the forest preserve, to Oneonta: left couple miles on 7, right, back onto 23

to 26 at North Pitcher; 26 to below Cincinnatus, 41 toward McGraw and
Polkville. At Polkville take 11 into Cortland. At Main St. half-right into
Tompkins, one block, I think to Prospect, right on Prospect, around up the
hill; the second intersection is the one where you have the right of way (or
that you have to look out for if following Plan One). A churchly building on
the left downhill side, then count the three houses. Or, first white one.
Where there's a will there're two ways at least. Usually. Maybe. You take
train, huh?

[UNTITLED]

We cannot agree

ever, quite, about

      the cats .

I cannot keep them by me, that close

sense, as I keep you and Carlos T., the anger

demand, needs, flow from you all, the love is

there, unequal always, never indifferent. Tangle

all this household in your mind, the kinds

of loving care we all give one another, all

      are necessary .

      And our two figures are

            set forth from Paris south,

      are set forth from Les Baux west and

      still return   .   Past that

      there are no more resurrections

           planned .

A week from now I put the garbage out again.

A week from now I give finals to my freshmen.

A week from now the kittens will be gone.

A week from now is payday — Joan,

you keep me sane   .   please

6 . I . 71

E.P. IN VENICE : REMEMBERING APRIL 1968, AND I SMILE

Eagle is old man .

We sit for a bit & smoke, look

out at the snow .

Old eagle never scream anymore, he

keep his silence . Say

two words now and then   .   Go

to the restaurant next door

or the café three blocks away

on the *canale* . sit

look out over the lagoon .   Old

eagle never smoke . never talk, never

drink but maybe a half-glass of wine with meals .

Hardly touched his soup.   Remembering this,

we sit for a bit & smoke, looking out, steal

glances at bare tree shapes, shadows .

Look out at the snow.

It's near noon .

It's January   .

17.IV.71

My shoes .

I have just taken them off,

                          my shoes.

Stare out the darkened window, damn, 've

forgotten the cigarettes in the car, empty

pack in my hand, crumple it, drop it in . 2 points

Have to put my shoes back on   .   they

look at me reproachfully from the floor

            laces loose . their

                tongues slack.

so scruffed already they are .

& had just relaxed

Cities & towns I have to give up this year

on account of my cancer: Amster-

dam, Paris, Apt, Saignon and Aix,

(Toulouse I'll never loose), Perpignan and Dax,

Barcelona and south

     (or the other way,

       Catania . I warn ya)

The hell, I read a review of a reading in January.

They loved me in Shippensburg, Pennsylvania.

Top of the 8th, after

four fouled off Gentry, still

2 and 2, a plastic bag

blows over home plate, Dave

Cash of the Pirates steps

  out of the box, steps

  back in, after speeding the plastic

    on its way

    with his bat, fouls

    two more off, then 3 & 2, then

infield bounce to the shortstop, out at first.

"Anything you want?"

      she asks, heading out the door, leading

      downstairs, get the bicycle out of the cellar .

—No, nothing, thanks. The slacks are brown, she is

carrying anything I want downstairs to take it for

a ride on the bicycle .

JOURNAL: APRIL 19 : THE SOUTHERN TIER

I

look out the window in upstate New York, see

the Mediterranean stretching out below me

down the rocky hillside at Faro, three

years, two months, fourteen days earlier .

8:25 A.M.

Rosemary gone back to sleep, pink & white . I

stand at the livingroom window drinking coffee, open

the doors to the balcony . Warmth beginning, tho

I wrap my hands about the cup, count

fishing boats in the sunglare, moving shoreward now

slowly, or

sitting there motionless on the flat sea .

a fat blue arm stretches out from the coast, ripples

where wind and currents show

muscle below the blue skin of sea

stretched out below me .

                            The coffee's

cold toward the end of the cup . I go

back to the kitchen for more hot . put

orange in bathrobe pocket, reach for knife, return

to the balcony with the fresh cup where the flat blue sea

fills my eye in the sunglare . stretches out below me.

The Southern Tier: the maple outside the window

warms in the early sun . red buds at the ends of branches

commence their slow bursting . Green soon

                        Joan moves

              her legs against mine in the hall, goes down to

start my egg . Carlos thumps the lower stairs . We move.

All our farewells al-

ready prepared inside us   .   aaaall our

deaths we carry inside us, double-yolked, the

fragile toughness of the shell . it makes

sustenance possible, makes love   possible

as the red buds break against the sunlight

possible green, as legs move against legs

possible softnesses   .   The soft-boiled

egg is ready now .

Now we eat.

19 . IV . 71

ALONG THE SAN ANDREAS FAULT

for Mark McCloskey

Low, mostly naked hills

dying scrub and rock

Juncture of Golden State and San Diego freeways

end of that american dream . Ghosts of

old insurance salesmen walk the ramps . Dairy

Queen and

taco stands in

valley flatlands

intersecting freeways insanely

landscaped by chickens in

constantly revolving baskets

The neon donuts blink . Other

side of the mountains / yr in the desert . Here

you really know it . Barry

Goldwater, Jr. is Congressman

These are his people .

JOURNAL : 20 . V . 71

When I had

finished the book

I could not remember your name, had

to turn, re

turn to the first page

to find who had written these poems .

        Fire on the mountain, light

        crossing a bridge between

        the twin peaks of death and

            the blind eye

        of God, your father　.　Burt,

never

the boat on the sea, never

the horse in the mountain .

    Blood in the dirt, Burt, Federico

    is dead,

& no one knew who he was .

        el barco sobre el mar

        y el caballo en la montaña .

y una aguja de luz en el centro

de tu cabeza, hombre　.

. . .

Carl is not coming to the reading . he has papers to correct

Marcia is not coming to the reading . she has a new baby

Joan is not coming to the reading . Carlos T. wants to

     play with the new baby & won't sleep

Walter is not coming to the reading because he thinks Carl will be there

     besides, Diane arrived today for a visit, and she

     was at the reading in Milwaukee yesterday

Gerth is not coming to the reading because he's behind time as usual

     and thinks that 9 o'clock is too late .

It's my reading . I take Marcia's mother to the reading .

A pleasant surprise, Mary and Ed are at the reading .

I forgot to get batteries for my cassette recorder today

     no one else records it .

I read until 10:30   .   It's a good reading.

. . .

LA LISIÈRE

How we move
about the wealth
of friendships :
too often at the edge of it

How rare, the move to center
    where we live

Selvage, that word,
each of us stands shyly
at the edge of woods

fearing the valley
chary of the sun
waiting .

Carl's eyes at parting, turning away, not
wanting to let go . We

all go the way we go

all the way . we

go, each his own

way . we all go

away . we go.

The tide runs high, the

evening star explodes .

What   is the sign

we mean to live by, we

mean, to live by . (?)

. . .

JOURNAL: JUNE, 1971   110 in the shade

Sitting in the tub
waiting for the ache in
my shoulders to go away

                    ·   nerves shlow down, the
                         muscles relax .

The tax is refunded in full .   I feel
the skinnyness of arms, the bony chest
cavity, front & back, as I soap up .

It's something else for the fingertips to remember
I haven't had a body like this since I was   15 .
What is it the ribs remember, the clavicles, the
            wingbones so unfleshed?
                To recognize the differences
in the quality of flesh tho, something else   .

                [+ +]

a doomed man planting tomatoes
backyard of a house he lives in
belongs to somebody else   . kneeling
on the earth
his hands move earth
feeling earth   .
                [+ +]

JOURNAL: JUNE 1971

TOP floor, then

when I look out, I look

out into the tree

outside .

            (This is not a
            plea for the economy)
                but

It's nice to think

(Carlos running & laughing downstairs

        Joan joking with him)

there is nothing we need .

"KITTY KAT!   PAPPI!"

      my son suggests,

      pounding at my door,

      lightly, tho .

"Where's your truck?"

          It

is not an alternative.

And the cat's in the

      laundryroom

          having supper .

            17/VI/71

JOURNAL : JUNE 1971

SHADOW   of a large bird
          floats
down the sunny half of the road
      runs west to east   .   We

here, under the shade of trees, south
      side of the street
wait for the lizard to come,
for the cat to arrive at the roof window
      calling for entrance .

We are hungry animals prowling this road.

I wonder, IS IT ALL LOVE?

We lie here in the shadow of the afternoon
        shadow of the bedclothes   slipped up .

Love & hunger   .   the bird

    the lizard, the cat,

           ourselves . Treecrown shadows

move over this half of the street, over
driveway and gutter.   down.

                   leaf shadow.

                         22 . VI . 71

JOURNAL: 26. VI. 71   THE NEWS

"TO THE REAR, HARCH! —to the

    right front, harch!"
                         (hup, 2—)

The blossoms

in the jar, the

petals on the roses are

beginning to fall to the table . The

wild flowers have sense enuf to close up tight

                  for the night .

    "GET THAT FORMATION TIGHT, CLOSE IT UP!"

We do .

The girls spread out on the sand

in the sun, half-

thinking, half-

listening to the remarks, half

asleep . Why move at all?

The sun.

keeps us talking

LOVE & DEATH

PLANTS NOW READY

Petunias, pansies, snaps, alyssum, early cabbage,
sweet spanish onions, LARGE selection of geraniums,
all colors, and perennials. Urns filled...

Urns filled with specifically precious, precious

What is it, Tim, we can fulfill

after specifically precious Death, we
speak to. Will I talk to you then, fill
yr/ ears with words . I want to

[Do not want that. Let
each man's words be his own.]

It

smiles at me

from underneath the table . That

green and yellow

ball .

Or what severances are offered?

what the doctors predict, what

the gods prescribe?

                  How can we

offer it all, Paul? how

ignore the earth movers . will

take it all down?

You ask a lot of questions tonite. Enuf of that .

                         The cats

move quietly about the house, lie

down where it is most comfortable

to lie   .   As

the goat bucks his leash, it snaps

tight, the

two-year length of that rope, tonite, love,

so buck I .

Figure that last year.   I want

to set it   .   year-after-next

            hopefully without pain

NOTHING I CAN'T STAND!

       I don't believe that either .

Let

the mountain be set

the house there forever

a final summer

gazing at the sun.

       Mediterranean .

[UNTITLED]

sundaysundaysundaysundaysunday

s u n

d a y

a quiet along the empty walks

single bird speaks to blue sky to

elm heavy with summer

E M P T Y   A N D   A L I V E

E M P T Y   A N D   A L I V E

E M P T Y   A N D   A L I V E

        The simple act of drinking a cup of coffee

        The simple act of pulling up one's trousers

buckling the belt . having shit, washed hands and face,

go to work . empty and alive . heavy with summer . light

with the promise of death . bright books in the bookcase,

window open, the day comes in, o fade the carcinoma, lay

down the two dollars, all those others rolling dice, but

it's my body, I'll bet on that . o, it floats thru the blood

with the greatest of ease . the pain goes and comes again . the

cat hunts in the grass, the gull swings over the sea, the blood sings a very old tune . Take it

easy, it's sunday, no?

All day.

27 . VI . 71

DOWN ALONG M–45

THE PARTICI-

          (pants are abt to descend)

pants are about to descend

July the 5th, this

Year of Our Nixon, 1971, upon

          Tom Jefferson

(within the infrastructure of

Grand Valley (Mich.) State College)

          for a festival of poesy!

Goodbye, minions of Dave Lorenz!

Hello, poets!

          PB
          Unofficial Greeter

JOURNAL: JULY 1971

Branches bend

in the wind, leaves

wave thru the window at me,

      and whistle .

I'm very popular today.

Gloria, Carlos T., and Joan

are down at Steve and Nancy's

Male cat comes in thru the window

      to talk to me. The

room is filled with evening light

3 hours yet to sundown. Hey!

      it's summer!

               20 . VII . 71

---

evening fantasy:

Traveling ahead again
in my head again
which cannot know that I'm dead again .
Beshit, fathered, and Magillicuddy
      am I?

People to talk with in those streets
      delight me
Spicer, I am not afraid :
Olson as a gigantic cherub
      garbed in nightgown, thinking;

Steve Jonas rolling happily for once in angeldust;
Kerouac writing the true novel of the Golden Eternity
on a ribbonless typewriter, without paper, never revising

Some /time7   finally to talk with Dr. Williams,
tho it seems I stammer,
he don't

> "if you like it, we
> like it too,
> we clued it with you"

and I, beyond all likelihood, get to that grove before Ezra,
walk about, saying:
> "I must prepare, I must
> prepare."

22.VII.71

Young, dying yellow birch on Owego St.
    half-block from the IGA .

fat black ants tool along beside me
or troll across the sidewalks . I am careful

Because I think maybe words are coming, I sit
on a stump in the sun in front of number 28,
staring at pink and white hollyhocks under its front windows,
an ambivalent paleness of hollyhock .
I always thought they were a
                somewhat gross plant,
                        those scratchy leaves .

The running samaritan this noon-hour, I've
delivered a bottle of freshmade orange juice iced, &
a suppository   25 mg. Adult .
insert one as directed for vomiting . and am
on my way
to the IGA
for cigs and a cold 6-pak of Coca Cola for Howard
to help celebrate
his first post-celebration-of-being-21 day .

Beware friends and well-meaning bar owners bearing gifts
that resemble three fingers high of excellent bourbon in a whiskey sour glass,
beware even the double shot . uh, *stark!*

On the way back to Tomkins St,
the ants accompany me in the hot sun. Don't
they know that sidewalks are terrible places to cruise,
for ants anyway?

And we always treated hollyhocks like
second class citizens, poor relations, bums, we
kept them out by the garage in back .
Those delicate blooms. The awkward stems. The hairy leaves.

23 . VII . 71

Index of Titles

DATE DUE

NOV 3 0 2004

GAYLORD			PRINTED IN U.S.A.